MW01290313

How Orchids Rebloom
Chuck McClung

How Orchids Rebloom

*An easy instructional guide
to happy reblooming orchids*

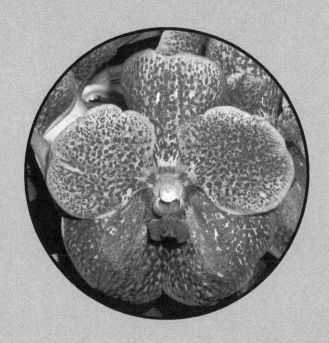

Chuck McClung

How Orchids Rebloom

First Printing 2019
Second Printing 2019
Printed in the United States of America.

How Orchids Rebloom
PO Box 371693
San Diego, CA 92137

www.howorchidsrebloom.com

CONTENTS

How to Use This Book   1

PART 1: REBLOOMING YOUR ORCHIDS
Chapter 1   How Orchids Rebloom   5
Chapter 2   The Five Main Reasons Orchids Fail to Rebloom   7
                Light   9
                Water, Fertilizer, and Humidity   16
                Temperature   33
                Pots, Potting Media, and Repotting   41
                The Orchid's State of Health *Before* You Received It   71

PART 2: KNOW YOUR ORCHID!
Chapter 3   Know Your Plant: The Native Habitat & The Growth Habit   81
Chapter 4   The Top 10 Common Groups of Orchids   100
                Cattleya Alliance   101
                Cymbidium   105
                Dendrobium   109
                Masdevallia/Dracula   115
                Oncidium Alliance: cool-growing   121
                Oncidium Alliance: intermediate- to warm-growing   125
                Paphiopedilum / Phragmipedium (Lady Slippers)   129
                Phalaenopsis   135
                Vanda Alliance   141
                Zygopetalum   145
Chapter 5   The Orchid Identification Tag   149
Chapter 6   Selecting and Caring for A New Orchid   161
Chapter 7   What Do I Do Now That My Orchid Is Done Blooming?   171

PART 3: ENHANCING YOUR EXPERIENCE WITH ORCHIDS
Chapter 8   Know Your Microclimates - Indoors and Outdoors   179
Chapter 9   The Origin of the Orchid Myth: 'Orchids Are Difficult to Grow' 189
Chapter 10 Diagnosing and Solving Orchid Problems   197

PART 4 - APPENDIX
Glossary of Terms   237
References   247

PREFACE

Plants have been a part of my entire life. As a wee lad, I tended the family backyard vegetable garden and mowed lawns in high school. After completing my Master's Degree in Botany, I worked in commercial greenhouses and retail nurseries, doing anything I could to learn more about plants. These days I lead seminars and workshops on a wide variety of gardening topics and advise others via garden and landscape consultations. My life mission is to help others solve their gardening dilemmas.

Working in large, independent garden centers and nurseries for many years really honed my skills helping others find happiness successfully growing and tending to their favorite plants.

Orchids are one such favorite plant for many people. Long ago I realized that most orchid books lacked what my customers *really* wanted to know. Answers to the common questions I encountered, like "What do I do when my orchid is done blooming?" were not to be found in books.

Over the years I have developed what I've been told is a simple, structured, easy-to-follow approach for growing and reblooming orchids. Many people told me that I should write a book. "But write it *the way you say it*," they said, "*not* the way it's written in other books."

Think of it this way: there are many "things" we have that "do something" if we follow the instructions. For example, you purchase a new food processor, and it comes with an instruction manual that tells you how to chop, puree, etc. If orchids were one of these "things" that are supposed to "do something" (i.e. thrive and rebloom) by simply following an instruction manual, it would be so easy. IT IS THAT EASY!

I've found that many people get overwhelmed or psych themselves out, because orchids are "alive," or they've heard that orchids are "difficult." *All you need to do* is (1) find out what kind of orchid you have, (2) learn about the environmental conditions your orchid experiences in its native habitat, and (3) reproduce those environmental conditions for your orchid, *and it must rebloom!*

IT IS THAT EASY! May this book be the instruction manual that helps you grow happy orchids and, more importantly, show you *How Orchids Rebloom*.

Have fun!
Chuck

HOW TO USE THIS BOOK

HOW ORCHIDS REBLOOM helps you clearly and quickly find the easy-to-follow information you need for your orchids to thrive *and rebloom*. After years of leading orchid classes, seminars, and workshops, I have found simple, effective ways to present the basics behind how orchids rebloom.

I like the expression, "Orchids are not difficult, just different." True. When we understand how orchids differ from each other AND how they are different from most other plants, it is much easier to understand the proper way to care for orchids. Most orchid books have a lot of "information" on how to grow orchids. It's commonly difficult to find answers to your simple questions like, "What do I do when my orchid is done blooming?" to "What do I do with all these roots growing out the top of the pot?" to "What size pot does my orchid need?" And let's be honest, what you really want to know is how to get your orchids to rebloom. Right?!

Therefore **PART 1: REBLOOMING YOUR ORCHIDS**, gets right to the point. **Chapter 1 How Orchids Rebloom** summarizes what you will need to do so that your orchids rebloom. **Chapter 2 The Five Main Reasons Orchids Fail to Rebloom** shows you how to provide what orchids need to rebloom, as well as how to avoid what prevents orchids from reblooming.

The chapters in **PART 2: KNOW YOUR ORCHID!** give the background information to help you better understand the basic ideas in **PART 1**. **Chapter 3 Know Your Plant** explains the growth habits and native habitats of the orchids we cover in this book. **Chapter 4 The Top 10 Common Groups of Orchids** describes the basic growing requirements and helpful hints for reblooming the ten most common types of orchids. **Chapter 5 The Orchid Identification Tag** helps you understand what some consider the most valuable part of your orchid, the identification tag. **Chapter 6 Selecting and Caring for a New Orchid** presents tips on how to buy the best orchid and what to do with a newly acquired orchid. **Chapter 7 What Do I Do Now That My Orchid Is Done Blooming?** answers one of the most common orchid questions.

In **PART 3: ENHANCING YOUR EXPERIENCE WITH ORCHIDS**, **Chapter 8 Know Your Microclimates** helps you take advantage of the small-scale differences in your indoor and outdoor environments so that your orchids thrive and rebloom. **Chapter 9 The Origin of the Orchid Myth** describes the history behind why many people still believe the erroneous notion that "orchids are difficult to grow." Ha! **Chapter 10 Diagnosing and Solving Orchid Problems** guides you through the basics of diagnosing problems you may encounter along your path to orchid mastery.

Throughout the book you will find **orange boxes** containing slogans of orchid wisdom. **Yellow boxes** summarize and review informational content These distillations are two of the most important parts of this book.

> orange boxes: slogans of orchid wisdom

> yellow boxes: informational orchid knowledge

In addition, most chapters end with a **Common Questions and Answers** section in which I answer all the common orchid questions I've been asked over the years. Use the Q & A sections to review the chapter or test yourself by trying to answer the questions before reading the answer.

This book is designed to be read front to back, yet each chapter can be read independently.

> **You only need to read chapters 1-4 to grow happy reblooming orchids!**

HOW ORCHIDS REBLOOM is also designed to help those who work in orchid-related retail settings (e.g. florists, garden centers, nurseries). By reading the orange and yellow boxes with the Questions and Answers sections, you will be much more informed helping your orchid customers.

By following my simple methods for getting to "know your plant," and for reproducing the native habitat of your orchid, I am quite certain you will have a thorough and working knowledge of *HOW ORCHIDS REBLOOM*. Enjoy!

PART 1
REBLOOMING YOUR ORCHIDS

CHAPTER 1
How Orchids Rebloom

CHAPTER 2
The Five Main Reasons Orchids
Fail to Rebloom

    Light

    Water, Fertilizer, and Humidity

    Temperature

    Pots, Potting Media, and Repotting

    The Orchid's State of Health,

        Before You Received It

CHAPTER 1
HOW ORCHIDS REBLOOM

All plants, and all organisms for that matter, have adaptations and *growth habits* that enable them to survive the environmental conditions found in their *native habitat*. When plants are grown outside their native habitat, they will only thrive and bloom when they experience those same conditions found in their native habitat: e.g. similar light, temperature, rainfall. Therefore, my number one favorite gardening slogan is:

Happy orchid growing on a tree.

> **The goal for *any type of gardening* is
> to reproduce the *native habitat* of your plant
> to achieve the desired *growth habit* for that plant...
> ...while having lots of fun. It's gotta be fun!**

Orchids grow *and rebloom* (i.e. the desired *growth habit*) when they experience the same environmental conditions found in their *native habitat*.

You might say, for instance, "Well, I don't think about the native habitat of my houseplants like my peace lily and philodendron. I just remember to water them, and they do fine." True. We often just have to remember to water our common tried and true houseplants like spider plants, philodendrons, snake plants, pothos, and they seem to do just fine.

This is true, because the indirect light and average room temperatures found in most homes *already mimic* the native habitat of most common houseplants: the understory of a tropical forest. Everyone has a suitable place in their home to grow the common houseplants, as long as we remember to water.

The best orchids *as houseplants* are therefore those that have a native habitat whose environment is similar to the location where you are growing orchids indoors. Similarly, outdoors we must find locations that reproduce the conditions found in that orchid's native habitat.

As we'll talk about later in the book, orchids are as diverse as plants themselves - some like sun, some like shade; some like it warm, some like it cool; some like it really dry, some do not like to dry out as much, etc. Some orchids will never rebloom as houseplants; some orchids will not survive outdoors year round, depending on where you live.

With regards to light, for instance, those orchids that receive a lot of direct sun in their native habitat will require a sunny location, indoors or outdoors, as long as other aspects of the environment are also met (e.g. not too hot, not too cold). Those orchids that grow in shady areas in their native habitat will thrive and rebloom in bright areas without direct sun.

For your orchids to rebloom, you will have to: (1) know what kind of orchid plant you have; (2) understand the environmental conditions found in that orchid's native habitat; AND (3) reproduce those environmental conditions for that orchid. If certain aspects of your particular orchid's native environment are missing, e.g. lack of light, too warm, too wet, your orchids will probably not rebloom. Therefore, with absolute certainty I will now proclaim:

> **All orchids fail to rebloom because some environmental attribute of their native habitat is missing, insufficient, or incorrect.**

FOR YOUR ORCHID TO REBLOOM, YOU SIMPLY NEED TO:

> **(1) Find out what kind of orchid you have;**
> **(2) Find out what environmental conditions**
> **your orchid experiences in its native habitat;**
> **(3) Provide the conditions found in the native habitat,**
> **AND YOUR ORCHID IS GUARANTEED TO REBLOOM!!!**

So, if your orchid has not rebloomed in the last year or two, it is very likely due to one of the five reasons described in the next chapter....

CHAPTER 2
THE FIVE MAIN REASONS ORCHIDS FAIL TO REBLOOM

INTRODUCTION

Orchids are long-lived, perennial plants. Annual plants like *Impatiens* and Marigolds, for instance, have only one year in which to flower and reproduce, and may do so even when quite stressed. However, long-lived perennials, like orchids, have the inherent ability to patiently wait to flower until next year, when and if conditions become more favorable.

Look at it this way. The production of flowers and the resulting fruits and seeds is the most "expensive" task for any flowering plant. If conditions are slightly unfavorable, an orchid can decide to "save its money" and spend resources on flowering when conditions improve.

"Why hasn't my orchid rebloomed?" I've answered this orchid question far more than any other. Over the years, I've found that there are five main categories of reasons why orchids fail to rebloom.

THE FIVE MAIN REASONS ORCHIDS FAIL TO REBLOOM:
(1) Light
(2) Water, Fertilizer, and Humidity
(3) Temperature
(4) Pots, Potting Media, and Repotting
(5) The Orchid's State of Health *Before* You Received It

All five reasons are interrelated. For example, how often you should water your orchid depends on the amount of light it receives, the temperature, and the size of the pot. As mentioned in the last chapter, these five factors directly correlate to the environmental conditions the orchid experiences in its native habitat.

**ALL ORCHIDS FAIL TO REBLOOM BECAUSE
SOME ATTRIBUTE OF THEIR NATIVE HABITAT IS MISSING.**

**If your orchid has not rebloomed
in the last year or two, it is likely that one or more
of the following five factors need attention!**

For each of the five reasons, you will find a **What To Know** section describing the background knowledge needed to provide the proper environment for reblooming orchids. Then you will find how to easily implement this knowledge with the section **What To Do.** Lastly, you will expand and reinforce your understanding of reblooming orchids with the **Common Questions & Answers** sections for each of the five reasons.

The easy Phalaenopsis, *or "Moth Orchid," is a great confidence builder on your path to orchid mastery!*

(1) LIGHT

LIGHT – WHAT TO KNOW

Light is the driving force behind almost all plants. How much light an orchid requires depends on how much light the orchid receives in its native habitat. Orchids that live in *full sun* in their native habitat will likely not rebloom if grown indoors with no direct sun. Orchids that never experience direct sun in their native habitat will suffer in a hot-n-sunny location.

I've seen many novice orchid enthusiasts get captivated by a particular orchid, bring it home, and never see it rebloom. They get discouraged, deduce they're "not good" with orchids, and give up. They could have been watering, fertilizing, repotting, and doing everything right, but all they had to do is *move the orchid closer to or farther away from the window*. You've probably heard the gardening expression, "right plant, right place."

The Proper Light Level

Light, or more specifically the *lack of light*, is a common reason many types of orchids fail to rebloom as houseplants. Many types of orchids (e.g. *Cattleya*, *Vanda*, *Oncidium*, see Chapter 4) require direct sun for at least part of the day, even during winter. Direct sun means sun actually hitting the foliage of the plant. Many homes lack a suitable location for these orchids. Even if you have sunny windows but place them on the coffee table ten feet from those windows, they will likely not rebloom.

Natural Light

Natural light (i.e. that bright, glowing ball in the sky) always works better for growing plants than artificial light. Ideally, orchids should be grown outdoors whenever possible to meet their environmental needs for light, temperature, air movement, etc. In temperate climates, however, orchids will need to spend at least part of the year indoors to avoid temperature extremes (summer heat and/or winter cold), depending on the orchid.

Indoors, windows that face south, southeast, or southwest will provide the greatest opportunity for natural light, assuming the windows are not obstructed by trees, eaves, walls, etc. North-facing windows may receive little or no direct sun at all. East- and west-facing windows receive natural light for only half of the day. A west-facing window receives afternoon sun, which may be too hot for some orchids. An east-facing window, on the other hand, receives morning sun during the cooler, first half of the day.

Depending on the construction, any window receiving direct sun for only an hour or two could collect enough heat to potentially "cook" an orchid. We don't want to cook our orchids. See Chapter 8 to help you better understand the indoor and outdoor microclimates in and around your home.

Windowsill gardens have their own microclimates of light and temperature.

Artificial Light

If your home lacks sufficient natural light for the orchids you wish to grow, you will need to provide supplemental, artificial light for those orchids to rebloom. Without going into a huge discussion on grow lights, here are a few important points.

I must first mention, somewhat humorously, the notion of home décor. Some people will simply not like having a grow light in their home. "It just doesn't go." If that is you, and you lack lots of light, stick with orchids that do not require lots of light, like *Phalaenopsis* and *Paphiopedilum*.

Hybrid light bulbs, LED banks, and high-efficiency grow lights are available to serious indoor plant-growing hobbyists. When selecting artificial lights for your orchids, be sure you understand the trade-offs between power output, energy consumption and heat output.

> **Some orchids require high light, some require low light; if they don't like the light they're receiving, they won't rebloom.**

LIGHT - WHAT TO DO

Indoors

Begin first by finding locations for your plants that require the most light. In any home there are far fewer high-light locations than low-light locations. Next, find suitable locations for those that require the next most amount of light and so forth.

Save bright, cooler, east-facing windows for those orchids that like bright, cool locations, like *Miltoniopsis, Paphiopedilum* and *Masdevallia*. However, use caution in east-facing windows that get really hot after only an hour of morning summer sun.

At temperate latitudes, the variation in day length changes dramatically over the course of the year. Both indoors and outdoors, you may need to relocate your orchids in spring and fall to ensure they receive proper light year round.

If you lack direct sun in your home, you will be most successful reblooming *Phalaenopsis* or *Paphiopedilum* orchids, instead of that purple *Vanda* at the garden show. Purchase orchids compatible with your home environment, and the orchid world will have snared another enthusiast.

Do some research before you run out and purchase a grow light. Understand the trade-offs between power output, energy consumption, and heat output. In regions with short-day winters, one of the best uses of grow lights is to extend the day length for your orchids. Supplementing winter days with 3-4 hours of artificial light starting in late afternoon helps the plant feel like it is experiencing a tropical winter day.

Phalaenopsis orchids are very easy to rebloom as houseplants, because our homes already mimic the conditions found in their native habitat. They prefer indirect light, and suffer in direct sun. *Everybody* has a space in their home suitable for a *Phalaenopsis* orchid to grow and rebloom!

Outdoors

All orchids, and really almost any plant, would prefer being outdoors as long as their needs for light, temperature, humidity, etc. are met. Outdoors, orchids experience *moving, fresh air,* another attribute of their native habitat (see Chapter 3) that is often missing indoors.

Outdoors provides the greatest opportunity for maximum sun. We can always reduce the amount of light a plant receives, but it's often more challenging to increase the amount of light. One of the best indirect light environments outdoors is the dappled light found under trees.

> **Understand the various light environments you have available for growing orchids, both indoors and outdoors.**
>
> **Know your plant, find the correct location for that plant, AND PUT THE ORCHID IN THAT LOCATION.**

COMMON QUESTIONS & ANSWERS
RELATED TO ORCHIDS AND LIGHT

Q: Do orchids need lots of light?
A: There are many kinds of orchids. Some orchids require lots of light to thrive and rebloom. Other orchids dislike lots of light and need protection from direct sun in order to thrive and rebloom. Know your plant! See Chapter 4 The Top 10 Common Groups of Orchids.

Q: Which kinds of orchids require a lot of light in order to rebloom?
A: *Cattleya, Dendrobium,* many *Oncidium, Vanda* and their relatives. See Chapter 4.

Q: Which kinds of orchids can rebloom without receiving lots of light?
A: *Phalaenopsis,* Lady Slippers (*Paphiopedilum* and *Phragmipedium*), *Masdevallia.* See Chapter 4.

Q: How do I know if my orchid is not getting enough light?
A: Know your plant - yes, I say it a lot. Many things *may indicate* lack of light.

Other factors may come into play. For instance, an orchid receiving less than ideal light is more likely to suffer from being watered too frequently.

An orchid receiving *insufficient light* may: not flower; *produce smaller leaves and growths than in previous years;* have darker green leaves than the same type of orchid in ideal light. A *Cymbidium* orchid with super dark-green leaves usually indicates that the plant is not receiving sufficient light. *Miltoniopsis* leaves, however, often look pale green when receiving proper light, and will fade to tan if it's too bright or too hot. Know your plant, and see Chapter 10 for more on diagnosing plant problems.

Q: How do I know if my orchid is receiving *too much* light?
A: Some symptoms of too much light can be: no flowers, lighter or paler colored leaves than the same plant in the appropriate light level, brown leaf tips. Some *Dendrobium* and *Phalaenopsis* orchids will develop a red edge on the leaf margin when receiving the most amount of light they can tolerate.

Sunburn typically occurs when a plant is placed in direct sun after having not experienced direct sun for an extended period of time (e.g. moved into direct sun after spending the winter indoors, or moved from total shade

The yellowish-white part of this leaf has been sunburned. Green parts of the same leaf indicate where another leaf was overlapping it.

under a tree into direct sun). Even plants that are native to desert-like environments with hot, direct sun can get sunburned when placed in direct sun after spending an extended period of time out of direct sun. Sunburned leaves turn light green to tan to almost white. One sign of sunburn occurs when a portion of an otherwise pale leaf remains green only where it was shaded by an overlapping leaf above it. See Chapter 10 for more on diagnosing problems with leaves.

Q: Can I use an artificial light to grow and rebloom orchids?
A: When the correct amount of artificial light is used (assuming all other environmental factors are met), any orchid can thrive and rebloom.

Q: What is the best light level for a *Phalaenopsis* orchid?
A: *Phalaenopsis* orchids prefer bright, indirect light - a light level similar to that required for an African Violet to thrive and rebloom. Years ago, I was taught a method for finding ideal light for a *Phalaenopsis* orchid called "The 12-Inch Rule." Hold your hand 12 inches from the leaf of a *Phalaenopsis*. A really sharp shadow of your hand indicates too much light. No shadow of your hand indicates not enough light. In ideal light you should see a slightly fuzzy, but distinct shadow of your hand on the leaf.

Q: I live in a climate with a very cold winter, so the *amount of light* that comes in my house and *where the light* comes in my house varies quite a bit over the year. How does that work for my orchids, and will they be confused from the fluctuating light levels?
A: The farther one moves from the equator, the greater the variation in both the day length and the angle of the sun over the course of the year. Depending on how your home is situated with respect to the sun, some orchids may indeed need to be moved a couple of times a year to adjust for this variation in light.

As winter approaches, move your orchids closer to the best source of natural light in the winter, assuming that location isn't too cold from a drafty window or too hot from a nearby heater vent. If you must grow your orchids in less than ideal light for a period of time during winter, try to provide the coolest temperatures they can tolerate.

As summer approaches, you may need to move some orchids away from the brightest, hottest windows. At latitudes far from the equator, some homes may actually receive more light entering windows during winter, because the sun is at a lower angle and not blocked by the eaves on the house or deciduous trees that have lost their leaves.

Q: I live in a subtropical climate. Can I grow orchids outdoors all year long?

A: Depending on your type of orchid, the answer depends more on the temperature extremes in your climate rather than light. For example, some subtropical climates may be too cold in the Winter for *Phalaenopsis* orchids, and too hot in the summer for *Miltoniopsis* orchids (see the section on "Temperature" below). In subtropical climates, you still may need to move your orchids a couple of times a year to meet their needs. Know your microclimates (see Chapter 8), and know how much light your orchids require (see Chapter 4).

One of the reasons that the Phalaenopsis *orchid is so popular and easy to rebloom, is that it does not require direct sun; everybody has a suitable indoor location for a* Phalaenopsis *orchid to thrive and rebloom.*

(2) WATER, FERTILIZER, and HUMIDITY

In the last section you learned how insufficient light is a common reason why certain types of orchids fail to rebloom. In this section we will discuss why *misunderstanding how to water is the most common reason orchids die.*

We must water / fertilize our orchids, and provide extra humidity in a way that mimics their native habitat. Failure to do so by watering the wrong way or fertilizing too much definitely prevents reblooming. Water, fertilizer, and humidity are all interrelated, and each will be discussed separately.

WATERING ORCHIDS – WHAT TO KNOW

Orchids, Water, and Nature

In nature, the orchids we're talking about do not live in "soil," as we typically think of soil. Most orchids (e.g. *Oncidium, Cattleya*) are "epiphytic"; that is, they *live in or on trees*, not in the ground. Other "semi-terrestrial," tropical orchids (e.g. *Paphiopedilum, Cymbidium*) live in shallow leaf litter on the forest floor, but definitely not *in soil.*

Orchid growing in its native habitat = on a tree!

By necessity, epiphytes and semi-terrestrial plants have adaptations that allow them to survive periods in which their roots "dry out." Therefore we must let our orchids "dry out" so that roots have access to the air they need.

Tropical habitat on the "orchid island" of Hawaii. Even though it frequently rains, orchids growing in trees receive lots of air.

In some tropical habitats, there may be periods of time in which it rains every morning, yet an orchid's roots will still dry out to some extent (i.e. have access to air) every day.

The root of an orchid is covered with a unique, spongy tissue called *velamen*. The function of the velamen is to *rapidly absorb small amounts of water and then quickly dry out.* If the velamen tissue does not dry out (i.e. does not receive air), the velamen begins to literally suffocate, decompose, and rot.

Orchid roots are covered with a firm, sponge-like, moisture-absorbing, tissue called velamen.

When any plant is "overwatered," the problem is not the excess of water but corresponding *lack of air,* resulting from too much water. If I asked you to sit at the bottom of a swimming pool for a few hours, you would not die from overwatering; you would die from lack of air.

> **Orchids like to "dry out" to some extent, because their roots need air.**
>
> **The roots of an "overwatered" orchid suffer not from an excess of water, but from lack of air.**

Orchids, Water, and Pots

When we grow orchids in pots we must ensure that the roots have access to air and dry out to some extent between waterings. To compensate for a root's need for both air and moisture we: (1) use different grades of potting media for different types of orchids (see the section on "Potting Media" below); and (2) water more or less frequently, depending on the needs of that particular type of orchid (e.g. time of year, growth habit).

The roots of an orchid in a plastic container will take much longer to receive the air they need than will the roots of the same orchid living in a tree. This doesn't mean that plastic containers are not good, It just means that *we must ensure the plant's roots sufficiently "dry out" (receive air) before watering the plant again.*

> **To reproduce the native habitat of our orchids,
> we must water our orchids based on
> their roots' need for both water and air.**

Why Orchids Get Overwatered

(1) Lack of information. Many people simply do not realize that most of the common, commercially available orchids require far less frequent waterings than common indoor plants. We water orchids less frequently than common houseplants so their roots will receive the air they require.

Different types of orchids require water differently.

(2) Watering according to a schedule (e.g. every Sunday) can be another reason that orchids suffer. As you collect more and more orchids (as you inevitably will after reading this book), you will find that different orchids, in different pots, in different types of potting media, will require waterings at different intervals. Furthermore, your orchids' needs for water change throughout the year. Orchids require more frequent waterings when they are growing leaves and the less when not growing leaves. We typically water more often in spring and summer and less often during fall and winter.

(3) The need to do something to the orchid, i.e. lack of patience, is another very common reason orchids suffer from too much water. There simply isn't that much to do with orchids. With respect to water needs, many orchids are a lot like cacti and succulents.

(4) When the pot has been sitting in standing water, an orchid can suffer from symptoms of overwatering. *Orchid pots should never sit in standing water.* A white-colored "salt ring" will develop around the bottom of a pot that has been sitting in standing water. When the pot sits in standing water, air cannot reach the roots through the drain holes in

Salt deposits indicate the pot has been sitting in standing water for a period of time. Not so good for our orchids!

the pot. Pot wraps or cache pots on gifted or store-bought orchids must be removed for long-term success. Let's summarize why orchids get overwatered:

> **Orchids do not like to be watered as frequently as other common indoor plants.**
>
> **Most orchids die because they are watered too frequently, and their roots fail to receive the air they need.**

Too Little or Too Much Water?

Like any plant, orchids definitely suffer if they do not receive enough water. When an orchid (or any plant) is lacking water, it is the oldest leaves that turn yellow and/or fall off first. When a plant is lacking water, the plant rids itself of its least valuable assets (i.e. the oldest leaves) and preserves the younger, newer

The oldest leaf is turning yellow on this Phalaenopsis orchid. Is there a need to be concerned?!

leaves for when, and if, conditions improve. See the section in Chapter 10 on "Diagnosing Problems with Leaves."

Some orchids have pseudobulbs, or water-storage organs that supply water to the younger, actively growing parts of the plant (see Chapter 3). When water and/or humidity is lacking, the *oldest* pseudobulbs shrivel or develop wrinkles as their stored water is used to support the youngest parts of the plant. However, when the *youngest* pseudobulbs and/or leaves appear damaged or discolored, something is definitely not right with the roots. When roots lack air, the plant cannot perform basic, simple functions, and the youngest parts of the plant suffer.

See Chapter 3 to understand pseudobulbs and how to easily discern the oldest leaves from the youngest leaves on your orchid plants. See also Chapter 10 Diagnosing and Solving Orchid Problems.

WATERING YOUR ORCHIDS – WHAT TO DO

How Often to Water Orchids

Orchids as epiphytes are better adapted to, as well as more easily survive, "not getting enough water" than "getting too much water." If you don't overwater them, orchids are pretty hard to kill.

Nobody can tell you how often to water your orchids. It would be mere guessing for me, or anyone, to make a blanket statement on how often to water your orchids without seeing your plants in their growing space. Watering frequency depends on the microclimates where you grow your orchids, e.g. light, temperature, air movement, type of orchid, size of pot.

> **WATER ACCORDING TO YOUR ORCHID'S INDIVIDUAL NEEDS**
> **An orchid in a plastic pot will need less frequent waterings**
> **than the same orchid in the same sized terra cotta or "orchid" pot.**
>
> **Orchids in smaller pots will need more frequent waterings**
> **than the same type of orchid in a larger pot.**
>
> **Orchids need more water when growing leaves**
> **and less water when not growing leaves.**
>
> **Water more frequently during spring and summer,**
> **and less frequently during fall and winter.**

"Once a week" works for many orchids, but it won't work for all of them. Ideally you check each one of your orchids every few days to see if they need water. As you get to know your different orchids, you will learn that some will need more watering attention than others. But still, how do you know *when to water*? How do you know when your orchids need water?

Lifting the pot and feeling the weight is one way to determine if the orchid needs water. Right after you water the plant thoroughly, it will weigh the most. The plant and pot will continue to get lighter as moisture is used by the plant or evaporated from the pot. Here, plastic pots are a great advantage, as opposed to clay pots, because they weigh very little; this creates a greater and more noticeable difference when the pot is wet versus dry.

Another method is to stick your finger in the potting media halfway down into the pot. If it feels wet in any way, do not water the plant. Choose a different place to stick your finger each time.

Alternatively, take a sharpened pencil or a clean chopstick, stick it in the pot for a moment, and remove it. If the potting media is still moist, a water stain will remain on the wood where the pencil has been sharpened. Again, choose a different spot each time to check for the need for water.

Avoid using plant moisture meters, which require direct contact with soil for best results. We do not use "soil" for the orchids we are discussing, therefore do not use a moisture meter.

> **Be patient.**
> **If you're not sure if you should water...don't.**

How to Water Orchids

Orchids are deliberately potted so that most of the water runs straight through the pot. This is a good thing. We want the water to drain freely, so the roots have access to air. Thoroughly *water the pot, and not the plant*. After watering, let the orchid sit until the water has drained, then put it back in its growing location. Watering a little bit at a time is not so good; roots do not get thoroughly wet, salts build up in the pot, and the plant suffers.

Do not allow water to sit in the folds of the leaves which can promote rot. It's always best to water orchids in the morning, especially indoors, so that any water that gets on the foliage has a chance to dry before evening.

Growing orchids outdoors provides air movement and reduces the risk that water on the foliage will damage the plant. Water in late afternoon or evening only when humidity is low, temperatures are warm, and air movement is good.

 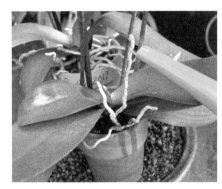

Water the pot...   *...not the plant.*

Large, deep humidity trays (see the section below on "Humidity") provide a reservoir to collect draining water. This reduces the number of trips to the sink, especially as you acquire more and more orchids - I'm sure you will after reading this book! The tray collects the water which then increases the humidity in the air around the plant. Do not fill the humidity tray so full that orchid pots sit in standing water; we want *pots on top of wet rocks.*

You may come across this silly idea of watering with ice cubes. "Just put a couple of ice cubes on the surface of the potting media once a week and let them melt." I advise against this method of watering for a few reasons. Remember our goal is to reproduce the native habitat of our orchids. I don't see much ice growing in the tropics, at least where the orchids we are talking about would be found in nature. Cold ice could damage or at least traumatize roots. One or two melting ice cubes a week can cause salts to accumulate in the pot and potting media, because water isn't flowing through the pot.

The idea of watering with ice cubes does work for a short period of time, however, which is all that many orchid buyers want from their orchid. "I'll just buy a new one; it's still cheaper than cut flowers" (see in the Appendix, "An Aspiration").

> **Water the pot, not the plant.**
> **Water thoroughly, not sparingly.**

Avoid Soaking Orchids

I recommend against soaking orchids or submerging the pot in standing water as a means of watering. Soaking the orchid can cause salts in the fertilizer or tap water to accumulate in the pot, which can harm the roots. Letting water flow over the roots and through the pot better represents what happens in nature and flushes out salts that can accumulate from fertilizer or tap water.

The only reason I ever suggest soaking an orchid occurs when an orchid potted in bark has become too dry. Really dry orchid bark does not readily absorb water. When watering an extremely dry orchid potted in bark in the usual manner, the water just runs over the surface of the bark and does not soak into the bark. Here, and only here, would I suggest soaking the pot for 20-30 minutes to allow the dry bark to thoroughly absorb water.

Watering a "Wilting" Orchid

When an orchid, or any plant, appears to be wilting, we typically think the plant needs water. And while that may be true, the appropriate question is, "Why is the plant lacking water?" Sure, most plants wilt when they are not getting enough water; they simply need more water. But with epiphytic orchids we may have a different situation.

Many times a "wilting" orchid (especially *Phalaenopsis*) does not need more water. Instead, it may have suffered from *overwatering* to the extent that *all the roots have rotted and died, leaving the plant with no means to uptake water...*until new roots have grown. If conditions do not improve (e.g. optimal humidity, water, temperature, new potting media) no new roots will develop, and the plant will die.

Before watering a wilting orchid, take the orchid out of the pot and inspect the roots. If the roots appear healthy and firm, the plant has likely become too dry. Give it a good watering, and be sure you are providing supplemental humidity.

On the other hand, if many of the roots appear rotted and dead, the plant likely needs to be repotted, and may even need a smaller container, depending on the orchid. You will find everything you need to

Living roots are white to whitish-green.

know about repotting orchids later in this chapter and more on diagnosing problems with leaves in Chapter 10.

> **When a plant is "wilting,"**
> **it does not necessarily indicate you need to provide water.**
>
> **An orchid may be wilting,**
> **because the roots died from too much water (i.e. lack of air).**
> **As a result, the plant is now wilting,**
> **because it lacks a means to uptake water.**

> **If your orchid appears to be wilting,**
> *take the plant out of the pot and inspect the roots.*

COMMON QUESTIONS & ANSWERS
ABOUT WATERING ORCHIDS

Q: How often do I water my orchid?
A: Nobody can tell you exactly how often to water your orchids. This very common and understandable question also requires the answer to its partner question, "How do I know when it is time to water my orchid?" (see next question).

I never make blanket statements about exactly how often to water anything. Watering frequency depends on your environment indoors and outdoors, type of orchid, size of pot, temperature, air movement, etc. If you don't overwater, orchids are pretty tough and hard to kill. If in doubt, don't water. Know your plant.

Water your orchids more often in spring and summer when they are growing leaves. Water less often during fall and water, when in bloom, or when not growing leaves.

Q: So, how do I know when it's time to water my orchid?
A: Ideally we would check each one of our orchids every few days to see if

they need water. The size of the pot and plant, the type of potting media, and air movement are some of the factors that affect watering frequency. Any orchid, like any plant, can die if allowed to dry out too much between waterings. Nonetheless, with orchids it's better to err on the dry side than on the wet side.

You can lift the pot and feel the weight as one way to determine if the plant needs water. Right after you water the plant thoroughly, it will weigh the most. The pot will get lighter as moisture is used by the plant or evaporated from the pot. Alternatively, you can stick your finger an inch or two down into the pot. If the potting media feels wet in any way, do not water the plant.

Q: Can I use my moisture meter to determine if my orchid needs water?
A: No. Avoid using a moisture meter. Orchids are typically grown in a potting media that is looser and faster draining than soil. A moisture meter may always read "dry" in such a loose potting media, which may then cause you to water your orchids too often.

Q: Is it okay to use tap water to water my orchids?
A: Tap water can be okay depending on the quality of the water that comes out of your tap, which can vary widely depending on your water source. Often excessive chlorine and salts in the tap water are not the best for orchids, especially lady slippers. Filtered water or distilled water is preferred. Many orchid enthusiasts have success using tap water, and that's just fine!

Q: How then does one actually water an orchid?
A: When an orchid needs water, it is best to water the pot thoroughly. Take the orchid to the sink, water the pot thoroughly, let it drain, and then put it back in its growing location. Most of the water will run right through the pot, and that is a good thing. Being epiphytes, we must provide potted orchids with a well-drained potting media, so the roots have easy access to air. Remember, we're trying to reproduce what orchids experience in nature, up in a tree where they regularly dry out.

Q: Can I water my orchid by letting it soak in water?
A: Preferably not. Soaking allows salts to build up in the pot. Instead, by letting the water/fertilizer mixture run through the pot, excess salts are flushed from the pot.

The only time I suggest soaking an orchid, occurs when an orchid potted in primarily bark or mounted on a slab got really dry between waterings (e.g. you went out of town for a couple of weeks). When bark is dry, it repels water; *pouring* water on it will not fully hydrate the bark. We want the bark to actually soak up water. Fully submerge the pot in water only (with no fertilizer) almost up to the rim of the pot for 20-30 minutes. You may need to weigh down the plant if it is trying to float on the water.

Q: My neighbor says she was told to just give the orchid a couple of ice cubes each week. Is that okay?

A: I advise against this method of watering for a few reasons. Remember, we are trying to reproduce the environmental conditions our orchids receive in their native habitat. I do not see a lot of ice growing in tropical climates, at least where the orchids we are talking about would be found growing. The cold ice could damage or at least traumatize roots. One or two melting ice cubes a week can also cause salts to accumulate in the pot and potting media, because water isn't flowing through the pot.

The idea of watering with ice cubes does, however, work for a short period of time, and that works just fine for some people. Like poinsettias, millions of orchids are grown annually as "disposable home decorations" (see "An Aspiration" in the Appendix).

Q: What do I do if my orchid looks like it's wilting?

A: Every orchid problem, like any plant problem, must be evaluated *on a case-by-case basis,* just like going to the doctor. There are just too many factors to say 100% for sure what to do if an orchid is wilting without further examining the plant. Here are some guidelines:

If your orchid looks like it is wilting, take it out of its pot and inspect the roots. If all the roots are healthy, firm, and spongy, give the orchid a good soaking in its pot as described above, and be sure you are supplying extra humidity. If the roots are soft and mushy, the plant may have suffered from overwatering (see also Chapter 10).

Orchids that have been severely overwatered often need to be repotted into the same size *or smaller* pot with fresh potting media (see the section below on "Pots, Potting Media, and Repotting"). Some orchids get overwatered and the roots or the whole plant rots to an extent that the plant cannot recover.

FERTILIZER – WHAT TO KNOW

The Need to Feed

In nature, most orchids and other epiphytic plants live in "low-nutrient" environments. Rainfall and the small amount of decaying organic matter that collects around the plant where it is anchored in the tree provide all the food the orchid ever receives and needs.

Therefore orchids, epiphytes, and other plants adapted to drying out in nature (e.g. cacti and succulents) thrive with little "food." That is why most succulent and orchid fertilizers are weaker or more diluted than other fertilizers. Lack of fertilizer is rarely the reason orchids fail to rebloom; too much fertilizer, however, can definitely prevent orchids from reblooming.

Unlike most potted plants living in soil, potted orchids receive very little nutrition from their potting media. Inert, inorganic or synthetic potting media, like lava or rock wool, provide no nutrition at all. While orchids grown in pots need little fertilizer, there still is the need for something.

Anything that is sold as a "fertilizer" must have on the label three numbers referring to the percentage of nitrogen, phosphorus, and potassium, also known as N-P-K, respectively. In very general terms, nitrogen (N) promotes leaf growth; phosphorus (P) promotes flower buds, blooms, and roots; potassium (K) helps overall functioning of a plant. Use a growth fertilizer, higher in the first number (e.g. 30-10-10), to provide extra nitrogen when your orchid is growing leaves. Right before or with the emergence of flower spikes, switch to a blooming fertilizer (e.g. 19-31-17), higher in the middle number, phosphorus.

People ask, "If I just want to use one fertilizer, which one should I use?" Select a "growth fertilizer" with proportionately higher nitrogen (i.e. first number highest), especially for *Phalaenopsis* orchids. Many orchids are potted with bark, moss, or other organic materials that break down over time. In the pot, the microorganisms are using nitrogen while decomposing the bark and moss, just like in your compost pile. It's best to supplement the spent nitrogen by selecting a fertilizer proportionately higher in nitrogen, like 30-10-10, for example.

> **Your orchids will be happier if you fertilize them according to the instructions on the package.**

FERTILIZER – WHAT TO DO

Orchids benefit from fertilizer for optimal health and reblooming. If you live in a region where your orchids grow outdoors, there may be enough nutrients in rainwater for your orchids to thrive with no supplemental fertilizing.

However, all organic-based potting media (e.g. bark, moss) will break down and decompose over time, *which uses nitrogen in the pot*; you must supplement this nitrogen loss.

There are many different ways to fertilize orchids. Select your favorite orchid fertilizer, read the entire instruction label, and *follow the instructions given on the package*. For many orchid fertilizers, you are typically dissolving small amounts of fertilizer (e.g. ¼ - 1 tsp) in one gallon of water. If you only have a couple of orchids, you can make a fertilizer mixture a gallon at a time and store it for future use.

I like to recommend watering every other time without fertilizer to flush out excess salts that may have accumulated in the pot. Lady slipper orchids (e.g. *Paphiopedilum*) especially suffer when salts build up in the pot. Never fertilize a really dry orchid, which can damage the roots. Instead, thoroughly water the potting media, then fertilize it at the next watering.

COMMON QUESTIONS & ANSWERS
ABOUT FERTILIZING ORCHIDS

Q: What kind of fertilizer should I use for my orchids?
A: Use a fertilizer higher in nitrogen (e.g. 30-10-10) when your orchid is growing leaves. Just before flowering and during flowering use a blooming fertilizer (e.g. 10-30-30).

There are many kinds of orchid fertilizers out there for you to choose from. Most importantly, pick one, read the entire instructions, and do what the instructions say.

Q: What do the three numbers mean on the package of fertilizer?
A: The three numbers on any fertilizer package refer to the percentage of Nitrogen (N), Phosphorus (P), and Potassium (K), in that order, N-P-K. In the most general terms, *Nitrogen* helps growing leaves; *Phosphorus* helps with growing flowers and roots; *Potassium* helps overall functioning of a plant. Read the previous question.

Q: How often should I fertilize my orchids?
A: Follow the instructions on the orchid fertilizer package for best results. Using more than what the package indicates can damage orchids.

Q: There is no instruction specifically for orchids on the fertilizer package. How do I know how often to fertilize and how much to use?
A: Use a different fertilizer if the package does not include an instruction specifically for orchids. Fertilizers not designed for orchids are often too strong for orchids.

Q: What if I just want to use one fertilizer?
A: If your orchid is potted in an organic potting media like bark, moss or a bark/moss mixture, use a fertilizer higher in nitrogen (e.g. 30-10-10). This extra nitrogen helps replace that which is consumed by the bacteria as they decompose the potting media, which is a normal, inevitable biological process.

      If your orchid is potted in an inert potting media like pumice, lava, or rock wool (see the section on "Potting Media" below), select a balanced fertilizer (e.g. 20-20-20).

Q: What are symptoms of using too much fertilizer or "fertilizer burn"?
A: "Fertilizer burn" or excessive fertilizer causes leaf tips and leaf margins to turn black or shades of brown. Another indicator of excess fertilizer is the presence of a white-colored salt ring around the bottom of the pot, the inside lip of the pot, or on the surface of the potting media.

Q: Should I fertilize my wilting orchid to help it out?
A: No. Never fertilize a really dry orchid. If your orchid is wilting, you will first want to find out why by inspecting the roots. If the roots look healthy and the potting media is dry, hydrate the potting media first. If the roots look dead, read the section above "Watering a Wilting Orchid."

Q: What will happen if I don't fertilize my orchid?
A: Your orchid will not die if you do not fertilize it. In nature, orchids typically grow in "low-nutrient" environments like in trees, on rocks, or in leaf litter. Lack of fertilizer will not prevent reblooming. If you do not fertilize your orchids they will produce fewer flowers / spikes and may not grow as large.

HUMIDITY– WHAT TO KNOW
The Need for Humidity and Fresh Air

Most tropical orchids experience a relative humidity greater than 50%. "Relative humidity" refers to the percentage of water vapor in the air, *relative* to the maximum amount of water vapor the air could hold at that temperature and pressure. Therefore, when it is raining, by definition the "relative humidity" outdoors is 100%. You can easily purchase an inexpensive *hygrometer* for measuring relative humidity.

Compared to indoors, tropical climates are not only more humid, but also more *breezy*. The various methods used to heat and cool most homes dries the air to a low relative humidity, often less than 20-30%. In our efforts to reproduce the native habitat of orchids indoors, we need to increase the humidity, especially when the heater or air conditioner is on.

One easy but horrible way to increase the humidity in the air is to place the orchid in a sealed plastic bag. However, this is ineffective, because the orchid will not receive *fresh air*. We must provide humid, moving, fresh air, which again reproduces what the plant finds out there in nature. Higher humidity (and temperature) creates the need for more air flow.

> **Fresh, humid, moving air reduces the risk of overheating and dries excess moisture from leaves and roots.**

HUMIDITY – WHAT TO DO

An easy way to increase the humidity for our orchids utilizes what are called "humidity trays." Simply fill a saucer or tray with small, wet rocks (e.g. pea gravel). The orchid plant is set *on top of wet rocks, NOT in standing water*. The water evaporates off of the rocks and creates a more humid microclimate around the orchids. Another type of humidity tray uses a plastic grate or grid that is held above water. Again, the plants are above the water, not sitting in water. Sufficiently large humidity trays can hold all the excess water that drains from watering pots, making for a lot less trips to the sink.

Avoid misting as a means to increase the humidity for orchids. The danger indoors is that water sitting for too long in the folds of the foliage can promote disease and rot.

A room humidifier, though not the home appliance for everyone, is another great way to increase the humidity in the air of the growing area. Avoid placing orchids near heater vents and air-conditioners both of which dry the air. Grouping orchids helps create a more humid microclimate around the plants. The larger the grouping, the more the need for air flow.

Humidity tray = a tray filled with wet pea gravel. The pot sits on top of wet rocks, not in standing water.

Remember ventilation! It's easy to create high humidity with little air movement. We want to mimic nature by providing the orchid with *moving*, humid air. If you accurately want to monitor humidity, purchase a hygrometer.

> **Provide moving, humid air.**
> **Try humidity trays with orchids sitting on top of wet rocks,**
> *not sitting in standing water*
> **Avoid misting your indoor orchids.**

COMMON QUESTIONS & ANSWERS
ABOUT HUMIDITY AND ORCHIDS

Q: Why do I have to provide extra humidity for my orchids?
A: Orchids are native to environments where the humidity is higher than in most of our homes, especially when the heater or air-conditioner is on. If orchids do not receive conditions similar to those in their native habitat, they may not rebloom. Outdoors, depending on the climate, you may not need to provide supplemental humidity.

Q: How do I provide extra humidity for my orchids?
A: Humidity trays are an easy way to increase the humidity for orchids. Place pots *on top of* wet pea gravel (or other small rocks) or on a grate. Do not let pots sit in standing water, which prevents air from entering the drain holes and reaching the roots.

Clustering orchid plants increases the humidity in the air around the plants. The larger the grouping, the greater the need for air movement. A room humidifier is another option for increasing the humidity for orchids.

Q: Should I mist my orchids?
A: Indoors, where air movement can be poor, avoid misting orchids. Water sitting in the foliage, especially overnight, promotes disease. Only if you have good ventilation, like outdoors or in a greenhouse, does misting become an option. Moving air prevents water from sitting on the foliage for too long.

Q: What are some signs that an orchid has suffered from low humidity?
A: Low humidity can cause the new, emerging leaves to stick together. Less than optimal humidity can also cause buds to fall off before opening, decrease flower life span, and cause new leaves to remain smaller than previous leaves.

Q: What are some signs that an orchid has suffered from misting?
A: As houseplants, when orchids are misted, water can sit in the folds of the leaves too long, promoting rot and decay. Usually the newest, emerging unfolded leaves are the most affected, because they are still so tightly folded up. Often the base of the newest leaf or two becomes soft and mushy, turns yellow or brown, and the leaf falls off at the base.

(3) TEMPERATURE

TEMPERATURE – WHAT TO KNOW

Temperature and an Orchid's Native Habitat

An orchid's temperature preference is a reflection of what that orchid experiences in its native habitat. Orchids are found all over the world in many widely varying habitats. Even within a small stand of tropical forest, the temperature, as well as light, will be much different at the top of the canopy versus in the understory. Therefore, some orchids will prefer warm, sunny locations, and some will prefer cool, shady conditions. The temperatures we provide for our orchids definitely impact how they rebloom.

Significant temperature variations occur within one stand of tropical forest: warmer in the sunny tree tops; cooler on the shaded forest floor.

Tropical orchids are typically organized into groups based on their temperature needs, cleverly yet appropriately named: **warm-growing, cool-growing,** and **intermediate-growing**. These three temperature groups correspond to, again, one specific attribute of an orchid's tropical, native habitat: elevation.

Those orchids native to lower elevations are the **warm-growing** orchids (e.g. *Phalaenopsis*). They generally prefer the consistently warm temperatures found in their native habitat. **Cool-growing** orchids (e.g. *Cymbidium*) are native to higher elevations and therefore require cooler temperatures, especially at night. Orchids with a native habitat at intermediate elevations are in the **intermediate-growing** group (e.g. *Brassia*). Pretty easy.

As an aside, terrestrial orchids native to temperate regions, or **hardy orchids**, are sometimes designated as a fourth temperature group of orchids. "Hardy" orchids (e.g. *Bletilla*) are so named, because in their native habitat they survive hard frosts and in most cases snow. For the purposes of this book, we are discussing tropical orchids and not the hardy orchids.

So how warm is warm, and how cold is cold? Think of your orchids' temperature needs in this *very generalized* way:

> **Warm**   Never < 60-65F / 15-18C; never > 90-95F / 32-35C.
> Average room temperatures typically work well.
>
> **Intermediate**   Never < 50-55F / 10-13C; never > 85-90F / 29-32C.
> Average room temperatures work well, not too hot.
>
> **Cool**   Never < 40-60F / 5-18C; minimum temperature
> required varies, depending on the orchid.
> Never > 80-85F / 27-30C; all resent heat.

There are no hard and fast lines with the three temperature groups, and you will likely find a lot of overlap. Few orchids will tolerate extreme heat (> 90F / 32C) for long without some consequence. At the other extreme, none of the orchids we're talking about will tolerate frosts.

Some orchids tolerate a wide range of temperatures (e.g. *Brassia, Cattleya*). What can be trickier are growing the orchids that prefer a narrow, more exacting range of temperatures. For instance, *Miltoniopsis* and cool-growing *Oncidium* orchids (formerly called *Odontoglossum*) quickly suffer when the air temperatures exceed 80F / 27C; they also suffer when the temperatures drop below 55F / 12C. Once again, this is a reflection of the more consistent, year-round environmental conditions found in their unique, native habitat.

Cooler at Night

Nowhere in nature is it warmer at night than it is during the day. Orchids prefer the temperature 10-15F / 5-8C lower at night. *High temperatures at night can cause problems.* During colder months, if you turn up your heater in the evening after you get home from work, your orchids may be confused and not rebloom. Growing your orchids outdoors or near an open window, whenever temperatures allow, lets them experience the natural temperature drop that occurs every night.

Cymbidium orchids, for instance, rarely rebloom as year round

This large, partly shaded, well-ventilated kitchen windowsill garden provides excellent humid microclimates in which the temperature drops 10-15F / 5-8C at night.

houseplants where temperatures are relatively constant throughout the day and the year. Growing *Cymbidium* orchids outdoors during frost-free months is absolutely essential for reblooming.

The Interaction of Light and Temperature

At a given elevation, more light results in higher temperatures. Just because your orchid requires lots of light, however, doesn't mean it will tolerate the heat associated with direct sun (e.g. *Miltonia*). Just because your orchid likes it cool, doesn't mean it will rebloom if grown in the shade year round (e.g. *Cymbidium*). Know your plant!

PROVIDE THE RIGHT TEMPERATURE – WHAT TO DO

Find out the range of temperatures your orchids prefer (See Chapter 4). Place your orchids in locations where they receive the temperatures they need. A thermometer is your key to measuring temperature fluctuations. Get a "maximum / minimum" thermometer to help you become familiar with the day and night temperature fluctuations in your orchid growing space (see Chapter 8 Know Your Microclimates).

This inexpensive, digital maximum / minimum thermometer records the daily high and low temperatures. The white box remotely monitors the temperature in another location and sends a signal back to the main unit.

How to Raise the Temperature

If you live in a climate that experiences frosts, then it will be necessary to protect your orchids or bring them indoors during winter months (or longer). Remember, however, as discussed above, most sources of indoor heat make the air drier.

A heat mat, often used for starting seeds, is a thick piece of sealed plastic with an embedded, electrical heating cable that you plug in. Most heat mats maintain the temperature 10-15F / 5-8C above ambient temperatures. Thermostats can help you more specifically regulate the temperature. Setting your plants on top of the heat mat will help the plant "feel" warmer.

How to Lower the Temperature

Cool-growing orchids (e.g. *Miltoniopsis*) suffer if grown outdoors where summer temperatures regularly exceed 85F / 29C. Indoors, home air conditioners dry the air as they cool it; provide supplemental humidity. In windowsill gardens, ventilation is required to avoid cooking plants. Open the window, or use a fan to reduce heat.

Growing your orchids outdoors, as long as temperatures, light, etc. allow, provides the easiest opportunity to provide a lower night temperature.

You may not have the means nor want to take the steps necessary to increase or decrease the temperature for your orchids. That is totally fine and dandy! The easiest way to grow orchids is to determine what range of temperatures and other environmental conditions you normally have in your space, and select orchids that prefer those conditions. Here is another reason why *Phalaenopsis* orchids make such great houseplants; they like the average room temperatures found in most homes!

Phalaenopsis orchids easily rebloom indoors as year round houseplants; they love average room temperatures and indirect light.

Learn the maximum and minimum temperatures your specific orchids require to rebloom.

FOR EASIEST REBLOOMING...
Learn the environmental conditions (e.g. light, temperature) you have in your orchid growing space.
Select orchids that prefer those conditions.

COMMON QUESTIONS & ANSWERS
ABOUT ORCHIDS AND TEMPERATURE

Q: Why do some orchids like cooler temperatures and some like warmer temperatures?

A: An orchid's temperature preference is a direct reflection of elevation in that particular orchid's native habitat. Those orchids that like it cooler are native to higher elevations. Those orchids that like it warm are native to lower elevations. Know your plant!

Q: Why do orchids prefer the temperature to be lower at night than during the day?

A: In nature it is always cooler at night than during the day, especially as the elevation increases. In our attempt to mimic what's happening in our orchid's native habitat, we must always provide cooler temperatures at night,

Cymbidium orchids rarely rebloom as indoor plants where light is lacking and temperatures remain relatively constant. Grow them outdoors whenever possible in frost-free conditions to receive the cool, fall temperatures they require to rebloom.

especially for "cool-growing" orchids native to higher elevations, e.g. *Cymbidium, Masdevallia.*

Q: What temperature should I provide for my orchid?
A: First find out which kind of orchid you have. Then use Chapter 4 to determine the range of temperatures your orchid needs for reblooming.

Q: During winter I turn down my heat while I'm at work, and turn it up a bit when I get home at night. Is that okay given what you said about cooler temperatures at night?
A: I haven't traveled the entire planet, but as far as I've seen, nowhere out there in nature is it warmer at night than during the day. Always try to provide orchids with a night temperaure 10-15F / 5-8C cooler than during the day.

Lady Slippers (Paphiopedilum, Phragmipedium) *will not rebloom in a hot location.*

Q: How do I know if my orchid is getting too hot or too cold?
A: Find out what kind of orchid you have, and then determine the range of temperatures it prefers (Chapter 4). Use a maximum / minimum thermometer to find a suitable location with the range of temperatures your orchid requires. Assuming all other environmental factors are adequate (e.g. light), put your orchid in that location.

Q: What are the signs that my orchid has been too cold?
A: Some of the symptoms that an orchid has been too cold are: soft, brown, *mushy* pseudobulbs; leaves or clumps of leaves break off at the base from soft, brown, black, and/or mushy spots. Many of the symptoms indicating that an orchid has been too cold are similar to those symptoms indicating that an orchid has been overwatered. See Chapter 10 Diagnosing and Solving Orchid Problems.

Q: What are the signs that my orchid has been too hot?
A: Some of the symptoms an orchid is receiving warmer than ideal conditions are: new leaves stuck together; pale green / yellowing leaves; brown leaf tips; wrinkled pseudobulbs. Remember that while these may be some of the signs that an orchid is too hot, these same symptoms could be indicating that another problem is present (e.g. wrinkled pseudobulbs may result from overwatering and root rot). See Chapter 10 Diagnosing and Solving Orchid Problems.

Phalaenopsis *orchids fail to rebloom in cold weather below 50F / 10C.*

(4) POTS / POTTING MEDIA / REPOTTING

As mentioned above, the orchids we're talking about do not grow in "soil." Some orchids live in trees, some grow in loose leaf litter on the ground, some even grow on rocks, but none in soil. Therefore, when it comes to pots and repotting, we do not treat orchids like common annuals and houseplants.

There are three main reasons we repot an orchid: (1) when the orchid has outgrown the pot and needs a larger one; (2) to replace the decomposing potting media; (3) trauma, when, for example, the neighbor kid's basketball smashes your *Cattleya.* Waiting too long to repot an orchid, repotting at the wrong time, using a pot that's too big, or using the incorrect potting media can prevent an orchid from reblooming.

I'll first show you **What to Know** about orchid pots, potting media, and repotting. I'll then put all this information together and show you step-by-step **What to Do** to easily and properly repot an orchid. Properly repotting an orchid (see below) also requires knowledge of the two types of orchid growth habits – monopodial and sympodial.

POTS – WHAT TO KNOW

Types of Pots

There are many different types of pots available for growing orchids: plastic, ceramic, terra cotta, pots with holes in the sides. With so many trade-offs, cost, durability, weight, decor, which is best for your orchid? Which kind to use?

So many pots. Which to choose?!

Many ask if orchids grow and rebloom okay in ***plastic pots***. Have you ever purchased an orchid *not* in a plastic pot? Sure, plastic pots work fine, *as long as the water easily drains out of the bottom/sides of the pot, so the roots receive the air they need.* Plastic pots are inexpensive, lightweight, and retain moisture. Orchid roots do not stick to the inside of plastic pots, providing for a less traumatic repotting experience. If you simply do not like the look of plastic pots, try "pot inside a pot." Set the plastic pot inside a decorative pot more to your liking, and water accordingly.

Orchid pots have holes in the sides that increase drainage and provide the roots with greater access to air. You'll water an orchid plant less often in a plastic pot than the same orchid plant in a similar-sized terra cotta or orchid pot. The disadvantage of orchid pots is that they can dry out too fast for certain types of orchids, in low-humidity environments, or with the forgetful waterer.

Don't like the look of plastic? Try "pot inside a pot." Avoid letting the pot sit in standing water!

Terra cotta would seem to be a nice choice for an orchid pot. Terra cotta looks great and breathes nicely for plant roots, keeping them cool. The big disadvantage of terra cotta pots, however, is that an orchid's roots securely adhere to the wall of the clay pot. When it is time to repot, many of the roots will break when removing the orchid from its pot. Also, terra cotta pots are heavy, cost a little more than plastic pots, and readily absorb excess salts.

A Dendrobium orchid loving life in a hanging basket.

Glazed ceramic pots work fine too. Be absolutely sure the pot has a large drain hole(s) to allow water to leave and air to enter the pot. Avoid glazed ceramic pots with one tiny (or no) drain hole which restricts drainage and prevents air from reaching the roots.

Orchids can be grown in **hanging baskets**, as long as the pot is the correct size (see the section below on "Proper Pot Size"). Orchids that have a hanging flower spike (e.g. *Dracula*) require a *slatted* hanging basket so that the pendulous flower spike can emerge from the bottom of the basket.

Reproducing the Native Habitat

You might ask, "If we are trying to mimic nature for our orchids, and our orchids grow in trees, why don't we just plant them in trees instead of using pots? Why not tie them onto logs or the trunk of a tree, and put some moss around the roots? Wouldn't that better mimic nature?"

Cattleya *relative mounted on a log...and reblooming!*

Yes! That would indeed better mimic nature. Outdoors or in a greenhouse, epiphytic orchids can be mounted on bark slabs, trees, or hanging baskets, as long as their environmental needs are being met (e.g. light, water, no frosts). Indoors, however, watering mounted orchids presents a challenge from a practical point of view. Outdoors we can just let the excess water fall on the ground; indoors we can't.

Indoors, mounted orchids dry out quickly during times of the year when your home is heated or air-conditioned. They will rebloom best in bathrooms or bay windows above a kitchen sink, for instance, because of the presence of extra humidity. That being said, any orchid can be mounted (vs. potted) if the necessary environmental conditions are met; for some orchids this is relatively easy (e.g. *Oncidium*), and for some it is not so easy (e.g. *Cymbidium*).

Proper Pot Size

The repotting process is stressful to the orchid (you'll see later), so we want to repot as infrequently as possible. Selecting the proper pot size, one that is neither too big nor too small, is especially important for the health and reblooming of your plant. Potting media naturally decomposes and needs to be replaced every few years. This is an inevitable fact and not a bad thing. Given that we will need to repot every few years, *we select a pot size that will accommodate only a few years of growth,* depending on the growth habit of your orchid.

A common mistake is selecting a pot that is *too large,* with the idea that it will give the orchid more room to grow. The potting media will decompose and the orchid will need to be repotted every few years anyway. Therefore, it just wastes a lot of potting media to give an orchid a pot that is larger than what a few years' growth requires. We also want to avoid "over potting," because the extra potting media prevents air from easily reaching the roots.

If the new pot is *too small,* the the plant will outgrow its pot, *before* the potting media needs replacing. Instead, minimize the disturbance to the plant by selecting a pot that accommodates just enough new growth, so that the orchid fills the pot right around the time the potting media needs replacing. The amount of additional space the new pot should provide is dependent on the type of orchid you have.

Orchids with a *sympodial* growth habit (see Chapter 3) grow "outwards" and get wider / larger. Select a pot size that provides space for 2-3 years growth. Some types of sympodial orchids simply create more mass per year (e.g. *Cymbidium, Miltoniopsis*) than do other types of sympodial orchids (e.g. *Dendrobium, Masdevallia*). Therefore, some orchids will require more space in their new pot than others do.

Orchids with a *monopodial* growth habit (see Chapter 3) grow "upwards" rather than "outwards." Therefore, select the *smallest pot* that into which the roots will comfortably fit, allowing no more than an inch all around the root mass (see more below). Many *Phalaenopsis* orchids will not need a larger pot when repotted. If there are a lot of rotted roots, a pot smaller than the original one may be required. An exception are the *Vanda*-type orchids whose roots require so much air that they do not need to have all their roots actually in the pot; some are even hung in pots without potting media or without any pot at all!

For sympodial orchids, provide a new pot that accomodates a few years' growth.

For most *monopodial orchids* (exception *Vanda*),
select the smallest pot into which
your orchid's roots will comfortably fit.

For *sympodial orchids,*
select a pot that will accommodate a few years' growth.

If the pot is *too small,* the orchid will outgrow the pot
before the potting media breaks down,
requiring repotting earlier than would have been necessary.

If the pot is *too large,* air is less able to reach the roots.
Potting media is wasted because it will have decomposed
before the orchid outgrows the pot.

COMMON QUESTIONS & ANSWERS
ABOUT ORCHIDS AND POTS

Q: Are plastic pots okay for orchids?
A: When I hear this question I jokingly ask back, "When is the last time you've seen an orchid for sale *not* in a plastic pot?" Sure, plastic pots are fine. As long as there are adequately sized drain holes in the plastic pot, *and you water accordingly*, plastic pots work fine.

Q: What are "orchid pots," and should I use one?
A: "Orchid pots" have holes in the side so that air more easily reaches the roots. While not required, orchid pots more accurately mimic nature for epiphytic orchids than do plastic pots and definitely reduce the chances of overwatering.

Semi-terrestrial orchids (e.g. *Paphiopedilum, Cymbidium*) and epiphytic orchids that require more consistent moisture (e.g. *Masdevallia, Miltoniopsis*) may dry out too quickly in orchid pots, especially those with large holes in the side. Not only can they dry out too quickly, but the finer grade potting media may fall out of the holes in the sides of the pot.

Q: Can I use terra cotta pots for my orchids?
A: Terra cotta pots are made of clay and "breathe," which keeps orchid roots cooler than when grown in plastic pots. However, orchid roots "stick" to terra cotta. When it comes time to repot, many roots break when removing the orchid from the pot. Far fewer roots are damaged during repotting when an orchid is grown in a plastic pot.

Q: What is the best kind of pot for my orchid?
A: As usual, the answer to this question depends on the type of orchid you have and personal preference. The main point is that we want to make our orchid feel like it is growing in its native habitat.

Most orchids could be grown in almost any kind of pot as long as their environmental needs, especially water and air, are met. That being said, *Cymbidium* orchids have large root masses and tend to like proportionately deeper pots than do other types of orchids.

I avoid planting directly into terra cotta pots (see previous question). Plastic or glazed ceramic pots with large drain holes work fine. All other things being equal, an orchid in a plastic pot will require less frequent waterings than the same type and size of orchid potted in a terra cotta or orchid pot. Indoors, when growing orchids that require more consistent moisture (e.g. *Miltoniopsis*), slatted baskets or mounted bark slabs are neither ideal nor practical, though not impossible.

Q: How big of a pot should I use? Should I use a larger pot?
A: Selecting an appropriately sized pot is another important component to successfully reblooming orchids. The pot size needed depends on many factors, e.g. type of orchid, size of orchid. A pot that is too large may retain too much water and prevent air from reaching the roots.

For *monopodial orchids* (see Chapter 3), a general rule of thumb is to select the smallest sized pot that comfortably accommodates the root mass. Sometimes you'll repot your *Phalaenopsis* into the same sized pot. An exception are some of the *Vanda*-type orchids. They have such potentially large root masses requiring lots of air, that slatted baskets are used, and in the right environment, sometimes without potting media.

For *sympodial orchids* (see Chapter 3), select a pot that allows for a few years' growth. The potting media should last longer than two years. Take advantage of that fact and provide a pot with enough space for your orchid to grow and fill the pot right around the time the potting media needs replacing.

Q: My *Cymbidium* orchid has a lot of dead pseudobulbs and hardly any living roots. You've said I'm supposed to use a pot that accommodates only a few years' growth. So doesn't that mean when I repot it I should use a smaller pot, because the plant is now smaller than it was?
A: Yes.

Q: How do I know if my orchid is in a pot that's too big?
A: If your orchid is blooming and looking happy, it is unlikely that the pot is too large. Remember the old saying, "If it ain't broke, don't fix it."

The only way to really know if your orchid is in a pot that is too big is to take the orchid out of the pot and see how large the root mass is. For instance, if your *Phalaenopsis* orchid has only two leaves and two short roots, a 12" pot is likely too large. Symptoms of overwatering can occur if the pot is too large, because air can't reach the roots as well (see the section above on "Water"; also see Chapter 10).

Q: How do I know if my orchid is "pot bound"?

A: The fear of the "pot bound" plant often stems from experiences with annuals, perennials, trees and shrubs purchased from less than top quality plant sellers. The notion of "pot bound," however, typically does not apply to epiphytic plants like orchids. Some orchids, like *Phalaenopsis* and *Dendrobium*, rebloom quite reliably in "smallish" pots because roots have easy access to air. Remember they live in trees. In fact, a pot that makes the plant appear "pot bound" may actually save the life of the orchid if you tend to water too frequently.

Instead, ask yourself, "Does my orchid lack room for new growth in its current pot?" or "Is the potting media decomposed and worn out?" If the answer is yes to either of these, follow the procedures described later in this chapter for repotting your orchid. If not, repot it at the appropriate time.

Q: How do I know if or when my orchid has outgrown its pot and needs a bigger one?

A: *Sympodial orchids* (see Chapter 3) grow laterally in one or more directions, and will definitely, at some point, fill their pot. If the newest growth is touching or hanging over the edge of the pot, the orchid needs a bigger pot. See more questions (below) on repotting sympodial orchids.

Monopodial orchids grow in one direction – upwards. Whether or not they need a bigger pot will depend on the particular type of orchid, the size of its root mass, and its general state of health. One indication that a *Phalaenopsis* orchid plant needs a larger pot occurs when the orchid is so big relative to the size of the pot, that it will not stand up on its own. Once the orchid plant is removed from the pot, select the smallest pot that comfortably accommodates the root mass. Sometimes a larger pot is required; sometimes a pot the same size is sufficient. Some *Vanda*

Please repot me! This Cattleya *orchid has definitely outgrown its pot.*

orchids never need bigger pot, because they love their roots hanging out of their pot or slatted basket, assuming humidity and other environmental factors are met.

Just because you've determined that your orchid needs a bigger pot doesn't mean that you should repot it immediately. If it's blooming or getting ready to bloom, do not repot it. Know your plant and the best time to repot it (Chapter 4).

Q: I've heard of people potting orchids in hanging baskets or in baskets made of strips of wood. Is that ok?
A: Sure, depending on the orchid and the growing environment. An orchid potted in a slatted basket is going to dry out way faster than the same orchid potted in a plastic hanging pot; this can be a good thing or a bad thing depending on the type of orchid, the environmental conditions you provide, and how you water.

Be sure that plastic hanging baskets have exceptional drainage. Some plastic hanging pots are designed to retain water and moisture for plants like tropical houseplants and trailing fuchsias, for instance. When using slatted baskets, be sure to provide optimal humidity for your particular orchid. Some orchids (e.g. *Vanda*) love slatted baskets, but quickly suffer when humidity is low.

Q: If we're supposed to be mimicking nature, then why don't we grow orchids on logs or slabs of bark or just stick them in a tree to help them feel like they're living in their native habitat?
A: You can. And it works really well if you can reproduce all the other aspects of the orchid's native habitat, especially temperature (i.e. no frosts or snow).

Practically speaking, an orchid mounted on a slab or log is more challenging to water indoors. After watering, the slab or log can continue to drip for a long time. On the other hand, when mounted orchids are grown outdoors or in greenhouses, you can just hose 'em down and let water run onto the ground or greenhouse floor.

Growing orchids in pots makes shipping easier for the commercial grower and easier "maintenance" for you when grown as houseplants. Certain orchids that require consistent moisture (e.g. *Masdevallia*) can be challenging to grow indoors mounted on slabs of bark or in trees, because they can dry out too quickly in the dry air of a heated or air-conditioned home.

Sure, in the proper environment you can definitely grow orchids in trees. Yeah, maybe not with duct tape though.

POTTING MEDIA – WHAT TO KNOW

What is Potting Media?

The tropical and sub-tropical orchids we are discussing are: epiphytes = living in trees, lithophytes = living on rocks, or semi-terrestrial = living in loose leaf litter on the ground, not in soil. *Therefore we do NOT use potting soil when repotting the orchids in this book.* Orchids are grown in a potting media that mimics the conditions found in their native habitat: something that drains exceptionally well but holds some moisture, depending on the particular type of orchid. The orchids you purchase are typically potted by the growers using their locally available materials: lava rock, Douglas fir bark, pine bark, redwood bark, moss, or bark/moss mixtures.

Orchids perform best in slightly acidic conditions. Most organic materials like bark and moss provide a slightly acidic environment for orchids. Inorganic or inert potting media may have a neutral pH, and should probably be avoided when strongly alkaline water is used.

Types of Potting Media

Orchid potting media can be thought of as two types: materials that decompose or deteriorate over time, and materials that do not decompose or deteriorate over time.

Decomposing Potting Media

Bark (Redwood, Pine, Douglas Fir) is one of the most readily available orchid potting media. It can be used alone or in mixes and has a slightly acidic pH. When really dry, bark needs soaking to fully rehydrate. Orchid growers typically have easy access to bark, depending on what trees grow in their region.

Sphagnum Moss is lightweight and slightly acidic. It quickly rehydrates and is commonly mixed with bark. Before repotting, be sure to mist the moss to reduce dust.

Coir or Shredded Coconut Fiber (sold under many different trade and brand names) is one of the newer potting materials to emerge in modern horticulture, not only for orchids but for general potting soil mixes too. Coir is the shredded husk of the coconut and is used like a peat moss substitute. It holds moisture well, and lasts longer than peat moss. Be sure to use the proper grade, from finely shredded to chunky.

Tree Fern Fiber is the chopped up trunk of tree ferns. It is long lasting and provides excellent aeration. It can be expensive and not as readily available as it once was.

Osmunda Fiber is the root mass of the terrestrial *Osmunda* fern. Also less common now than it once was, it is very tough and durable and holds well over 100% of its weight in water.

TYPES OF DECOMPOSING POTTING MATERIALS

Coconut fiber

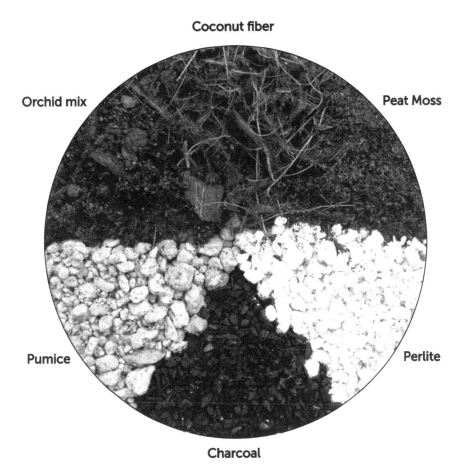

Orchid mix

Peat Moss

Pumice

Perlite

Charcoal

TYPES OF NON-DECOMPOSING POTTING MATERIALS

Non-Decomposing Potting Media

Perlite is a superheated volcanic ash mineral; it's an inexpensive, light-weight potting media additive that provides excellent aeration and drainage with some moisture retention. Be sure to select the proper grade, depending on the needs of your orchid.

Pumice is superheated volcanic rock. It is slightly heavier than perlite, provides excellent aeration and drainage, and has better moisture retention. Again, select the appropriate grade.

Lava Rock provides excellent aeration; because it is inert, provide a balanced fertilizer. Water quality is also important, and alkaline water may not grow the best orchids. Larger grades of lava rock dry out very quickly; use it only when growing orchids in high-humidity environments.

Rock Wool is melted rock that is spun into fibers resembling a sponge. It provides excellent aeration while holding lots of water. It is used as an additive in orchid potting mixes.

Charcoal is another additive used in orchid potting mixes. Made from heated hardwood, it provides aeration and can filter salts and substances in the water.

Use the potting media you feel most comfortable with. Some find it easier to determine if it's time to water when the orchid is potted in moss. Some like the look of bark better. Generally speaking, the type of potting media used is often determined by personal taste. You must also select the correct size or grade of potting media for your orchids. See the next section.

Size or "Grade" of Potting Media

Orchids grow in many different habitats in nature. Some habitats have more moisture, humidity, and rainfall; some habitats are rather dry. To compensate for different orchids' needs for moisture and air, we use different "grades" of potting media. The grade of potting media refers to its fineness or coarseness; it is the most important factor in determining which type of potting media you select, which is again based on the environment in your orchid's native habitat.

Most orchid potting media and potting mixes will indicate the grade on the package. You may see wording like "fine," "medium," "large," or "coarse" grades. The package may even list which orchids are suitable for that particular grade.

The chart on page 55 shows which grade of potting media each of the Top 10 groups of orchids needs for reblooming. Select finer grades for orchids requiring more consistent moisture for their roots (e.g. *Miltoniopsis*

GRADES OF ORCHID BARK:
Fine < 1/2"; Medium 1/2"-1"; Large > 1"

"Large" Bark

"Medium" **"Fine"**
bark **bark**

and *Masdevallia*). Select coarser grades for orchids whose roots need more access to air (e.g. *Phalaenopsis, Vanda*). Orchids that live in loose leaf litter (e.g. *Cymbidium, Paphiopedilum, Epidendrum*) require a "semi-terrestrial" mix typically consisting of a mixture of fine bark, compost, pumice, or chunky coconut fiber, depending on the brand.

> The appropriate "grade" of potting media serves to mimic
> the amount of moisture and air
> an orchid's roots receive in its native habitat.

ORCHID POTTING MEDIA PREFERENCE CHART

	Semi-Terrestrial	Fine	Medium	Large
Cymbidium	X			
Epidendrum	X			
Lady Slippers	X-------------X			
Zygopetalum	X-------------X			
Masdevallia / Dracula		X		
Miltonia / Miltoniopsis		X		
Odontoglossum		X		
Oncidium Alliance		X-----------X		
Cattleya Alliance		X-----------X-------------X		
Phalaenopsis		X-----------X-------------X		
Vanda			X-------------X	

(see more in Chapter 4)

COMMON QUESTIONS & ANSWERS
ABOUT ORCHIDS AND POTTING MEDIA

Q: What is the best kind of potting media for orchids?
A: The type of potting media you select is often determined by personal preference or what materials are locally available. You also have to select the correct "grade" of potting media for your particular type of orchid.

The potting media you select depends on the type of orchid and is a direct reflection of the orchid's roots' needs for moisture and air in its native habitat. See the Orchid Potting Media Preference Chart above, refer to Chapter 4, and know your plant!

Q: What does the "grade" of the potting media refer to, and why is that important?
A: The potting media "grade" refers to its fineness or coarseness, and is the most important factor for determining which type of orchid potting media to use. Select a grade of potting media that correlates with the air and moisture

needs for your particular orchid.

Finer grades have smaller "pieces" and therefore smaller air spaces that retain more moisture, preferred by orchids like *Miltoniopsis* and *Masdevallia*. Larger or coarser grades of potting media drain more rapidly, giving roots more access to air. *Vanda* orchids are one extreme example that require a coarse, chunky potting media so that the roots quickly have access to air immediately after watering.

Q: What kind of potting media should I use for my *Phalaenopsis*?
A: A medium-grade potting media (not too fine, not too chunky), or moss, or some kind of bark/moss mixture. If you have a young *Phalaenopsis* requiring a pot less than 4" in diameter, use fine bark.

Q: A friend just gave me one of his/her old orchids. How do I know if the orchid is potted with the appropriate potting media?
A: Know your plant! Find out what kind of orchid you have. Then consult the Orchid Potting Media Preference Chart above, and see Chapter 4 to determine which grade of potting media your new baby prefers.

Q: A friend just gave me one of their old orchids. How do I know if the potting media is still good?
A: A musty or moldy smell in the pot may mean that the potting media needs replacing. If the potting media looks more like soil or feels excessively soggy, it likely needs replacing. A salt ring around the bottom of the pot indicates that the pot has been sitting in standing water, which speeds the decomposition of the potting media and causes root rot.

The presence of little black flies buzzing around the potting media, likely fungus gnats, may be a sign that the potting media has decomposed and needs replacing.

Q: There are little mushrooms growing in my orchid's pot. Is that okay?
A: The presence of mushrooms usually indicates that the potting media is decomposing and needs replacing. The presence of mushrooms does not create an emergency situation, but offers the suggestion to repot the orchid at the next suitable time to do so.

REPOTTING ORCHIDS – WHAT TO KNOW

Why Repot?

There are three main reasons you will at some point need to repot your orchid. First, some orchids, like other potted plants, simply outgrow their pot. Second, you will eventually need to replace the decomposing potting media. As the potting media decomposes, it becomes more like soil and less like the well-drained material it once was. The third reason to repot an orchid results from a trauma or injury to the plant. An orchid may need repotting if it suffered from overwatering by the house sitter while you were on vacation. If your dog's tail sent the orchid flying off the coffee table, you'll be repotting it.

When to Repot

As you will see below, the repotting process can be extremely stressful to the plant. Therefore, we want to repot as infrequently as possible to minimize the disturbance to the plant. Yet we still need to repot every few years to refresh the potting media.

If an orchid is not repotted, poor drainage resulting from decomposed potting media causes the roots to rot from lack of air, often resulting in symptoms of overwatering. We want to repot **before the potting media has fully decomposed**.

Orchids with a sympodial growth habit will definitely fill their pot over time. They will need to be repotted **before they grow over the edge of their pots**. Orchids with a monopodial growth habit on the other hand, sometimes do not need a bigger pot when repotting (see Chapter 3 for more on sympodial and monopodial growth habits).

Spring and summer are generally the best times to repot an orchid. More accurately, the best time to repot an orchid is not based on the seasons but on what the orchid is doing or where the orchid is in its annual cycle of growth. For almost all orchids, **repot as new growth (leaves, roots) begins**.

> **WHEN TO REPOT ORCHIDS:**
> *before* the potting media has decomposed;
> *before* the plant grows over the edge of the pot;
> as new growth begins, usually spring and summer.

When Not to Repot

Avoid repotting orchids **during fall and winter months**, especially in the temperate latitudes. The shorter day length may not provide enough light for the orchid to quickly rebound from the stress of the repotting event.

Avoid repotting **if your orchid is blooming**. "If it ain't broke, don't fix it." Repotting an orchid and disturbing the roots may cause the buds and blooms to fall off (see the section in Chapter 10 on "Bud Blast").

Furthermore, avoid repotting **if the new growths or pseudobulbs are almost fully grown or mature**. At this point in their annual cycle of growth, most orchids are getting ready to rebloom; repotting may prevent reblooming.

One exception to the rule of repotting "as new growth begins" relates to the growth habit of *Zygopetalum* orchids. They create flower spikes *as new leaves emerge, before the pseudobulb forms*. It's best to repot *Zygopetalum* orchids after flowering (See *Zygopetalum* in Chapter 4).

WHEN *NOT* TO REPOT ORCHIDS:
fall and winter;
when growing buds, blooms, or flower spikes;
if new growth is almost mature;
...if you don't know what kind of orchid you have.

BEFORE REPOTTING YOUR ORCHID:
Know which kind of orchid you have;
select the correct grade of potting media;
sharpen and sterilize your clippers;
water the plant.

REPOTTING ORCHIDS – HOW TO DO IT!!!

What You'll Need to Repot Your Orchid

When it's time to repot your orchid, find a nice, easy-to-work-in space, and be ready to make a small mess. Gather all your supplies first: the new pot, new potting media, clippers, garden gloves, something to sterilize your clippers (e.g. flame, alcohol). ***Water your orchid before repotting it***; moist roots are less brittle.

Always sterilize your clippers with a flame or alcohol before cutting anything! Sterilization prevents transmitting diseases from plant to plant. Failure to sterilize clippers is by far the most common reason orchid viral infections are transmitted from plant to plant. Sterilize your clippers each time before repotting or cleaning a different orchid.

Also *be sure your clippers are sharp.* Dull blades damage surrounding plant tissue. We want swift, clean, sharp cuts, and this is true for any type of pruning, dividing, or trimming any plant. Now comes the brave part!

THE FIVE STEPS TO REPOTTING AN ORCHID:
1. Carefully take the orchid out of the pot.
2. Remove all the old potting media.
3. Remove anything dead: leaves, roots, pseudobulbs.
4. Position the orchid in its new pot; slowly add new potting media.
5. After repotting, replace the ID tag, and water thoroughly.

Next are the details step by step:

---

1. Carefully take the orchid out of the pot.

First, remove the plant ID tag, set it aside, and don't lose it! The ID tag is very important (see Chapter 5 The Orchid Identification Tag).

Gently grasp the plant from the base and wiggle it to begin removing it from the pot. Be careful with roots which may be stuck to the sides of terra cotta and ceramic pots. Orchid roots are pretty tough, but they are brittle and not accustomed to being handled this way.

If the plant won't budge, try gently squeezing plastic pots to loosen the root ball a bit. You can also stick a long knife between the root ball and the side of the pot to loosen it a bit. Some ceramic pots, especially those in which the opening at the top of the pot is smaller than the widest part of the pot, may need to be broken to remove the plant.

Mounted orchids that have outgrown their bark slabs may not need to be removed from their slab. Instead, a new slab can be placed under or adjacent to the previous slab, and the orchid simply continues growing.

Step 1: Phalaenopsis *orchid removed from its pot (left);* Cymbidium *orchid removed from its pot (right). For thick root masses, begin to remove potting media (**Step 2**) by starting at the bottom center of the root mass.*

2. Remove all old potting media.

Begin removing old potting media. Gently squeeze the root ball and let a lot of the old potting media fall away. Healthy, vigorously rooted orchids (e.g. *Cymbidium*) create a huge root mass, and removing all the potting media may take some time. With massive or tight root masses, it works best to begin by gently massaging the bottom center of the root ball instead of on the sides. Pruning away dead roots as you remove old potting media often makes the process easier.

As mentioned above, the

Step 2: *Remove all the old potting media.*

best time to repot is typically just as new growth begins. New roots are associated with new growth; take special care not to damage any of the newest, young growth tips and roots.

Step 2: *When removing old potting media, be careful not to damage young roots (arrows).* Phalaenopsis *(left) and* Oncidium *(right).*

3. Remove any dead roots, leaves, pseudobulbs, etc.

Once all the old potting media is removed, prune away any dead roots, leaves, or and any other dead parts of the plant. Remove dry leaf bases wrapped around pseudobulbs. Even with the best of care, orchids typically have a few dead roots, usually the oldest roots. Dead roots are limp and soft, or dry and shriveled. Living, healthy roots are full and firm; look for a bright, shiny root tip. The new roots grow from the youngest parts of the plant and should be the healthiest.

For *monopodial orchids,* the oldest roots are attached lowest on the central "stem." If the lowest part of the central "stem" is dead and decayed, it too should be removed with a sharp cut.

For *sympodial orchids,* the roots that grew from the oldest pseudobulbs are often the dead ones. If almost all of the roots are dead, I like to leave a couple of dead roots to help anchor the plant in its new pot.

Prune away mushy, dry or otherwise dead pseudobulbs. Do not remove leafless, living (firm and

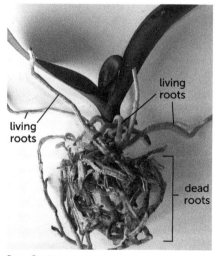

Step 2: *Old potting media is removed.*
Step 3: *Remove all dead leaves and roots. Most of the lower part of the root mass is dead. A few living roots are at the top.*

hard) pseudobulbs. Leave them on the plant to provide water to the younger, actively growing parts of the plant. Rinse the plant to remove any remaining soil.

Apply a powdered fungicide to major cuts to prevent disease and infection. My orchid mentor always suggested cinnamon powder, yes, regular old ground cinnamon, as a natural bactericide and fungicide; apply to any cuts made on orchid plants. It works!

Step 3: Phalaenopsis *orchid all cleaned up and ready for its new pot. Yes, it's ok!*

4. Position the bare-root orchid in its new pot and slowly add potting media.

When reusing any pot, be sure to thoroughly wash it first. Adding some sort of drain material (e.g. large bark, large gravel, broken pottery) to the bottom of the new pot is especially important for large specimen plants or when using columnar-shaped pots. Heavier drain materials like broken pot chards or rocks will make the pot bottom-heavy and less likely to topple over. However, heavy drain materials in the pot make it more difficult to "lift the pot" as a means to determine if the plant needs water, because there will not be as much of a difference in weight when the pot is dry versus when it is wet.

Now it's time to properly position the cleaned up, bare-root orchid in its new pot. Monopodial and sympodial orchids have different growth habits (see Chapter 3), so we must position them differently in their new pot.

Positioning Monopodial Orchids

Monopodial orchids grow in one direction - upwards. Therefore, position them *in the center of the new pot*, so that the base of the lowest, healthy leaf is level with the eventual surface of the new potting media.

Positioning Sympodial Orchids

Sympodial orchids, on the other hand, grow laterally or outwards, like most perennial garden plants. Younger sympodial orchids typically create new growths along one unbranched rhizome.

Position young sympodial orchids with the oldest growths and/or pseudobulbs at the edge of the new pot. In this way the plant has the opportunity to grow *across* the pot. If the plant is positioned in the center of the pot, the subsequent new growths reach the edge of the pot more quickly. As a result, you have to repot sooner than would have been required. Large specimen plants or plants with new growths on several sides of the plant, however, should be positioned, like most potted plants, centered in its new pot.

Position a symarodial orchid so that the *base of the newest growth* is level with the surface of the new potting media. A proper repotting of a sympodial orchid may therefore result in the oldest pseudobulbs being buried a little in the new potting media, and that's okay.

Step 4: *Properly position the orchid in its new pot. Monopodial orchids (left - Phalaenopsis) are centered in their new pot. Sympodial orchids (right – Oncidium) are offset with the oldest part of the plant against the edge of the new pot and the youngest growth in the center of the pot.*

Once your orchid is positioned in its new pot, slowly and gently add potting media a little bit at a time. Be sure to mix packaged potting media before using it in case finer particles have settled to the bottom of the bag. Carefully tuck bark chips or moss around roots starting at the bottom of the pot, and work your way up the pot. Avoid "pouring" potting media into the pot.

Step 4: *Once properly positioned, slowly add small amounts of potting media.*

Adding large amounts of potting media at once will result in a "wobbly" repotted orchid, because the potting media hasn't been evenly distributed between roots. In addition, the resulting air gaps in the pot can cause the plant to dry out too quickly in the future.

As you work your way up the pot, use your fingers, chopsticks or other probe to help the potting media fill into the spaces between the roots. At the same time, use caution not to damage roots. Periodically tap the bottom of the pot on the table to help the potting media settle in snug around the roots.

Be sure to consistently maintain proper positioning of the plant as you add more potting media.

> *Monopodial* orchids should be positioned
> with the base of the *lowest leaf*
> level with the top of the potting media.
>
> *Sympodial* orchids should be positioned
> with the base of the *new growth*
> level with the top of the potting media.

All done! Phalaenopsis *orchid (left) centered in its new pot with the base of the youngest leaf level with the top of the new potting media;* Oncidium *orchid (right) offset in its new pot with the base of the newest growth level with the top of the new potting media.* **Step 5:** *Replace the ID tag, and water thoroughly.*

5. Replace the ID tag and water thoroughly.

Immediately after repotting, *replace the ID tag!* Write the date you repotted the orchid on the ID tag, on a separate tag, or in a journal. Then thoroughly water the pot *without fertilizer;* some sediment will drain through the pot, which is okay. Continue to water thoroughly until the water that drains out of the bottom of the pot is clear.

Aftercare

The repotting process can be tough on fragile, brittle roots; those bruised and broken roots need a chance to heal after repotting. Wait a little longer than usual for the second watering. Bruised and broken roots rot quickly in a constantly damp environment.

Provide less than optimal light for about a week, especially if the plant had a lot of dead roots or the plant was severely stressed. If the orchid has suffered severe root loss and only one or two roots remain, use a clip or stake(s) to stabilize the orchid in the pot.

AFTER REPOTTING

1. Replace the ID tag.
2. Water thoroughly without fertilizer.
3. Provide less than normal light for a week or so.
4. Wait a little longer than usual before watering a second time.

Dividing Orchids

You never *have to* divide an orchid. There are only a few reasons you must divide an orchid: (1) the plant has grown too big for the space you have and you need a smaller plant; (2) you want to propagate it to give away, or sell parts of the plant; (3) the orchid is growing "all wonky." Some epiphytic, sympodial orchids (e.g. those with long rhizomes) can grow in all sorts of directions, including way up above the pot; here, dividing may be necessary to ensure that all parts of the plant grow into new potting media.

Monopodial orchids have one growth; they cannot be divided. However, if they reach a sufficiently large height, the top part of the plant can be removed and repotted in a new pot. Sometimes *Phalaenopsis* and *Vanda* orchids will create a "side branch" that once sufficiently large, can be removed and potted separately.

Sympodial orchids are easily divided once they reach a certain size. There is no specific rule on where to divide an orchid; it depends on how that orchid has grown, the position of pseudobulbs, new growth, etc. *Maintaining a minimum of five growths or pseudobulbs per division* enables the orchid to rebloom later that same year without skipping a beat. This means you may need to wait for several years to divide the plant you just bought last month at the grocery store. If you divide out and repot just one or two pseudobulbs, you could be waiting for a few years for your new division to rebloom.

Make all cuts with sharpened, sterilized clippers. Again, we want swift, sharp cuts to minimize tissue damage (just like in surgery), not ripping and tearing. The best time to divide an orchid is also the best time to repot it, just as new growth begins, usually spring and summer. Dust all cuts with a powdered fungicide or ground cinnamon to prevent disease.

Depending on the orchid, dividing may require only the careful cutting of one rhizome. If you know in advance that you will be dividing your orchid, you can cut the rhizome at the place of division weeks or months before the actual repotting. In this way the plant is given a chance to heal and create new roots well in advance of the stress of repotting. For large specimens, dividing may involve an axe, shovel, or machete, not kidding! Just whack it into pieces!

After reading this chapter you now know
why orchids need to be repotted
at the proper time,
using an appropriately sized pot,
and the proper "grade" of potting media.

THE FIVE STEPS TO REPOTTING AN ORCHID:

Before repotting: water your orchid; sterilize and sharpen your clippers.

1. Remove the orchid from its pot; save the ID tag.
2. Remove all old potting media.
3. Remove dead leaves, pseudobulbs, and roots; rinse the plant.
4. Position the orchid in its new pot; begin adding new potting media.
5. Once repotted, replace the ID tag, and water thoroughly.

COMMON QUESTIONS & ANSWERS
ABOUT REPOTTING ORCHIDS

Q: When is the best time to repot my orchid?

A: Spring or summer is generally the best time to repot orchids. Repot as new growth begins and before they have outgrown their pot. Again, know your plant; there are exceptions. Avoid repotting orchids from fall through winter, especially in cold climates. With shorter winter days, there may not be enough day length for the orchid to adequately recover from the stress of repotting. If your orchid is blooming, wait to repot it.

An excellent time to repot this Cymbidium *orchid. New growth has just begun, and the previous year's growths have just filled the pot.*

Q: Why do I have to repot my orchid every few years?

A: Many orchids are potted with organic materials like moss or bark to mimic what the roots experience in nature: excellent drainage with some moisture retention. These organic materials will naturally decompose over time (there is nothing you can do about that) and will become more like soil and less like the well-draining potting media it was originally intended to be. Therefore orchids must be repotted every few years, and the old potting media must be replaced with fresh potting media.

Some inert potting media, like pumice, lava rock, or rock wool will not decompose over time. Orchids potted in these materials will only need repotting once they've outgrown their pots.

Q: When should I NOT repot my orchid?
A: Avoid repotting orchids:
> 1) when they are blooming;
> 2) fall and winter;
> 3) if you're not sure what kind of orchid you have (see Chapter 4);
> 4) if you're not sure how to repot an orchid (re-read this chapter).

Q: Why am I not supposed to repot my orchid when it is blooming?
A: Properly repotting is stressful to the plant. You won't kill your plant by repotting it while in flower or spike. However, disturbing the roots at this time may cause the flowers and/or buds to fall off (see Chapter 10 on "Bud Blast"). If your orchid is blooming, there is no need to repot it.

Q: I just bought an orchid that is blooming, but I don't like the pot it is in. Can I repot it?
A: You can repot it. A proper repotting won't kill the plant, but the flowers may not last as long because of the disturbance to the roots. Be patient and repot it after it has finished blooming. If you absolutely can't stand the pot, try setting the plant with its undesirable pot inside a more preferable pot.

Another alternative is to carefully slip the orchid out of the current pot and set it in the new pot, without disturbing the root ball; tuck moss or bark in the space between the root ball and the pot to stabilize it.

Q: A friend just gave me an orchid. How do I know if the orchid needs repotting or if the potting media has decomposed?
A: A musty or moldy odor in the pot is a good sign that repotting is necessary. If there is barely any potting media left in the pot, or if the orchid easily falls out of the pot, it needs repotting.

A salt ring around the bottom of the pot indicates that it has been sitting in standing water for at least some period of time, which is not good for the plant. Take the orchid out of the pot and inspect the roots. If the roots are healthy, put the orchid back in the pot. If the roots look dead, repotting the orchid is required (see Chapter 2).

The person who gave you the orchid may have repotted it themselves using an improper potting media. First identify the orchid, then refer to Chapter 4 to help you determine which grade of potting media the orchid prefers. If it's in the wrong potting media, go ahead and repot it at the appropriate time.

Q: My daughter was practicing her air guitar and knocked my orchid off its stand so that it fell out of its pot. Even though it's the middle of winter right now, should I repot it?

A: Yes. This is an exception to the rule. Definitely and immediately repot your orchid if your dog, the wind, pet tarantula, or an asteroid knocks it out of its pot.

Q: What are the differences between repotting orchids with a monopodial growth habit versus repotting orchids with a sympodial growth habit?

A: For a detailed explanation, see above "Repotting Orchids - What To Know," and see the section in Chapter 3 on "The Growth Habits of Orchids."

A *monopodial orchid* grows in one direction, upwards. It is positioned in the center of its new pot, which may not need to be larger than the previous pot. Monopodial orchids are often positioned a little lower than they were in their previous pot, with the base of the oldest leaf level with the surface of the new potting media.

A *sympodial orchid*, on the other hand, increases in size and grows "outwards," usually requiring a larger pot. Position sympodial orchids with the oldest part of the plant at the edge of the pot, so that the plant has space to grow *across* the pot. If we repot them like monopodial orchids, in the center of the pot, the plant will grow to the edge of the pot sooner, before it's time to replace the potting media. Large specimen orchids with new growths on many sides of the plant are positioned in the center of the pot.

Position your sympodial orchid with the *base of the newest growth* level with the surface of the potting media. A proper repotting of a sympodial orchid may result in some of the oldest pseudobulbs being buried in the potting media, which is okay.

Q: Can I / How do I mount a potted orchid on a slab or in a tree?

A: First, do steps 1-3 for repotting an orchid. Take the "bare root" orchid and spread the roots out evenly on the slab or on the tree. Place moss on top of the roots. For smaller orchids on slabs or logs, wrap fishing line around the plant and entire slab or log to secure the plant. For larger orchid on slabs or in trees, one can use "finishing" nails to provide a secure support for the fishing line. Soak the slab thoroughly after mounting and with each watering.

Most importantly, know your plant. Some orchids do not like to be mounted because mounting does not mimic their native habitat (e.g. most *Cymbidium* orchids). Mounted orchids can be very unforgiving if you do not maintain the proper humidity, moisture, and temperature. Mounted orchids require more frequent waterings than the same orchid in a pot.

Q: When I repot my orchid, what do I do with all these roots that are growing out of the top of the pot? Do I cut them off?

A: Remember that most of the orchids we're talking about are epiphytic and live in trees. They produce roots that may grow in any direction looking for a tree trunk or something to "grab" onto.

I've noticed this tendency for some people to want to cut off the long stringy roots that grow out of the top of the pot. Don't. There is no reason to cut off the (healthy) roots; doing so will only stress the plant. The presence of many roots *outside the pot* may indicate that the plant is unhappy *in the pot*. A plant that has been overwatered, for instance, may produce roots outside or on top of the pot, because all the roots inside the pot have died.

When it is time to repot the orchid, carefully tuck those roots back into the pot. I actually like to leave one or two of the roots sticking out of the pot, so I can see the active, growing root tip. Watching the tips of the roots gives you a powerful tool to assess the health of the plant. Healthy root tips look fresh, shiny, bright green or pink to burgundy. Root tips that are dry, brown, or black indicate a problem.

Q: When do I have to divide my orchid?

A: You don't ever have to divide your orchid if you don't want to. You might choose to divide your orchid for a couple of reasons. For example, you may want to give away or trade a piece of the plant. Alternatively, you may decide to divide an orchid if it has grown too large for the space you have for the plant. That is, you simply want a smaller plant. Some orchids can grow to an enormous size. If you want to accommodate the size of the plant and keep finding larger pots, there is no need to divide it. Usually only sympodial orchids are divided. *Phalaenopsis* orchids are rarely divided because there is nothing to divide.

(5) THE ORCHID'S STATE OF HEALTH, *BEFORE YOU RECEIVED IT*

IS MY NEW ORCHID HEALTHY? – WHAT TO KNOW

Receiving an orchid that is already in a poor state of health is the fifth common reason orchids fail to rebloom. That stressed orchid you received from your neighbor who has given up after trying for four years, or that sad one on the sale rack at the grocery store, may be in such a poor state of health that even under the best of conditions it may take a year or two, or more, for it to rebloom.

Making Flowers is Expensive

Annuals like *Impatiens* and Basil have only one year to grow, create flowers, and produce seed. When you go on Summer vacation and the house sitter forgets to water your outdoor containers, you'll come home to find your annuals near death but still producing a flower or two.

Orchids, on the other hand, are long-lived, perennial plants. Being perennial plants they can wait to rebloom if conditions are less than ideal. Creating flowers and the subsequent fruit and seed is the most "expensive" task a plant can perform. An orchid is in no hurry to create that fantastic flower if

Like raising kids, creating flowers is expensive!

conditions aren't just right. What's the rush? It may decide to say, "I have a headache this year."

With a stressed orchid, you can provide a perfectly correct environment, and it still may not rebloom right away. The plant could be in such a sad state that it could take a year or two, or more, in those improved conditions for it to fully recover and rebloom.

Stressed Orchids You Purchase

In the world of commercially grown and sold orchids, there are typically a few parties involved: the grower, the wholesaler, the shipper, and the retailer. Obviously the growers are doing everything right, otherwise we wouldn't have orchids to buy. Growers that are also retailers are a treasure; they will offer you orchids in near perfect health. What happens between the time the orchids leave the growers and reach you can really take a toll on the plants.

Most orchids are shipped from the grower to either a distributor or to a retailer. In transit, their buds and flowers get bumped around, and orchids can sometimes sit in a truck for several days, often in total darkness. In addition, they may experience less than ideal temperature and humidity, especially during the coldest parts of winter and hottest parts of summer. Once they are taken off the truck, you inherit these stresses.

That's a lot of Phalaenopsis *orchids for sale!!*

However, shipping stresses can be relatively minor compared to what often happens after the orchid arrives at the retailer. These days orchids are a staple item in many box stores and grocery stores, and it is here that orchids experience an entirely different set of stresses.

Orchids in chain and box stores are stressed all the time. All the different kinds of orchids are displayed in the same location in far less than ideal conditions, e.g. no direct sun anywhere, low humidity. The staff rarely knows anything about orchids. Moreover, rarely does anyone water them, and when they do get watered, they are usually watered improperly, e.g. water sits in the folds of leaves or remains in the pot wrap.

Some retailers display orchids right by the front door to catch your eye; during winter, cold drafts impact the orchids as doors open and close several times a minute. These conditions alone may prevent them from reblooming right away no matter how ideal the conditions are that you provide once you get them home.

Whenever possible, purchase orchids from local, independent nurseries or from *local growers* at orchid shows. The orchids are properly cared for and staff members actually know how to assist you. That being said, even at reputable nurseries, orchids experience mishaps, and make it to the sale rack in a less than ideal state of health. Be ready to practice patience when buying discounted, out-of-bloom orchids. See Chapter 6 Selecting and Caring for a New Orchid, and Chapter 10 Diagnosing Orchid Problems.

Local orchid shows are an excellent place to buy orchids.

Orchids sold during winter, even if from an orchid grower or quality nursery, may experience a little stress going from a high-humidity growing environment to a lower-humidity, heated home. During winter, get those newly purchased orchids home as quickly as possible, and provide supplemental humidity.

Stressed Orchids You Inherit

Many of us have received an orchid from a family member or a neighbor who has given up on the orchid or is convinced they are just not good at growing them. (How about buying them this book and an orchid as a pick-me-up gift?!) Sometimes the orchid was in an otherwise excellent state of health and was simply lacking light. Maybe it was overwatered, and some of the roots have rotted. The orchid may have even experienced a combination of several stresses in its less-than-ideal conditions.

Problems sometimes occur when you inherit an orchid that had been repotted by a previous owner. Many perceive their orchid in its "little pot" as "pot bound" and decide to repot it. Unaware that orchids are epiphytes, the orchid gets repotted into a pot that is too large, or is repotted with potting soil or some other inappropriate mix that will, at some point, ultimately cause the plant to die.

RECOVERING A STRESSED ORCHID – WHAT TO DO

After a couple of years of less than ideal care, an orchid may require a year or two or more in optimal conditions to restore its health to a point in which the orchid is capable of reblooming.

To begin the recovery process, look for the ID tag and try to identify the orchid. You'll need to know what kind of orchid you have to provide the proper light, temperature, potting media, etc. See everything above and Chapter 4. Know your plant and provide proper light and temperature as well as

Should I buy one of these sale orchids?!

moving, humid air.

How do the youngest leaves appear versus oldest leaves? Take the orchid out of the pot and inspect the roots. If the roots and potting media look fine, there is no need to repot it right away. However, many inherited orchids need immediate repotting.

In the future, when someone gives you an orchid that they are "giving up on," here are a few questions to ask the "donor": Where did she get it? Did she inherit a stressed plant, buy it off a sale rack, or buy it brand new in bloom at a nursery / store? How long has she had it? The longer she's had it, the longer it may take for it to rebloom - yikes! Have she ever repotted it? If so, how long ago? What size pot was it in before it was repotted it? What potting media did she use to repot it?

> **A stressed orchid that has suffered
> in less than ideal care,
> may take awhile to rebloom
> once given the best of care.**

> **To assess the health of your stressed orchid,
> take it out of the pot and look at the roots.**
>
> **If the roots and the youngest leaves look healthy,
> the orchid has the capability to recover.
> If all the roots are dead and/or the youngest leaves look bad,
> your orchid may take quite a while to recover, if at all.**

> **Orchids appreciate patience.**

COMMON QUESTIONS & ANSWERS
ABOUT AN ORCHID'S PRIOR STATE OF HEALTH

Q: A friend just gave me this orchid. How do I take care of it?

A: The first step in properly caring for your orchid is to identify it. If you don't know what type of orchid you have, you will not know if it needs lots of light or cool temperatures, for instance. As I say over and over, "Know Your Plant."

Look for the ID tag in the pot. Without an ID tag, some orchids cannot be definitively identified without flowers on the plant (see Chapter 4). However, an experienced orchid enthusiast can often steer you in the right direction, perhaps identifying it to the proper genus or alliance. Take the orchid to your local orchid club or society meeting or independent garden center, and have a specialist look at it.

Once you know what type of orchid you have, refer to Chapter 4, and determine what conditions the orchid prefers in terms of light, temperature, frequency of watering, potting media, etc.

Q: A friend just gave me this orchid. How do I know what type of orchid it is?

A: Look for the ID tag. If there is no ID tag, see the answer to the above question.

Q: A friend just gave me this orchid that has not rebloomed for them for several years. Should I repot it?

A: First identify the orchid; then see Chapter 4. Then ask yourself a few questions: Is it in an appropriately sized pot with the appropriate grade potting media? If not, take it out of the pot, inspect the roots. If the pot, potting media and roots seem okay, then ask: Do the youngest leaves appear to be healthy? Are any of the youngest or oldest pseudobulbs wrinkled? If only the oldest pseudobulbs are wrinkled, that can be okay.

If only the youngest pseudobulbs or leaves are wrinkled / discolored, or soft / mushy, that's not so good; you may need to repot it. Re-read the above sections in this chapter and read Chapter 10 Diagnosing and Solving Orchid Problems.

Q: How do I know if the roots are healthy?

A: Take the orchid out of the pot and inspect the roots. Soft, mushy or dry, roots are dead; firm, grayish-white to whitish-green roots are healthy.

Q: Someone just gave me this orchid. How do I know if it has bugs?
A: If there are no flowers, there are likely no aphids present. Look for clear sticky patches on the leaves, which may indicate that an insect pest is present. Look for white "cottony" fuzz on the leaves, in the folds of the leaves, on the ID tag, and around the rim of the pot; this may indicate the presence of one of the most difficult pests to eradicate - mealybugs (see the section in Chapter 10 on "Pests"). Take the plant to your local independent nursery or garden center and have them take a look at it. They will be able to suggest a suitable remedy like a Neem Oil-based product or an Insecticidal Soap, depending on the critter.

Q: I like to rescue sad orchids. What should I watch for when I buy a discounted, out-of-bloom orchid from a sale rack?
A: I like to emphasize buying orchids with ID tags; start by looking only for sale orchids with ID tags.

To best assess the health of the plant, discern the youngest from the oldest parts of the plant (see Chapter 3). If only one of the oldest leaves is yellow, I wouldn't be alarmed. However, if any of the youngest leaves or

The youngest leaves on this discounted Phalaenopsis *aren't saying, "Take me home."*

pseudobulbs look damaged, discolored, or disfigured in any way, skip it; don't buy it. If the youngest parts of the plant seem okay and in good health, go for it! See also Chapter 6 Selecting and Caring for a New Orchid.

For *Phalaenopsis* and other monopodial orchids, select one in which each newer leaf is larger than the previous leaf. For a given type of sympodial orchid, select the one with the largest and most pseudobulbs. Orchids with several healthy, emerging new growths are often a good bet too.

The new growth on this discounted Cymbidium *orchid looks brown and rotted at the base. Don't buy it! See Chapters 6 and 10 for tips on discerning (un)healthy orchids.*

Q: I just got this orchid from a friend, and she said it hadn't rebloomed in several years. How do I get it to rebloom?
A: First, positively identify the plant. Second, see the first question in this section. Third, start reading this book from the beginning.

PART 2

KNOW YOUR ORCHID!

CHAPTER 3
Know Your Plant:
The Native Habitat & The Growth Habit

CHAPTER 4
The Top 10 Common Groups of Orchids

CHAPTER 5
The Orchid Identification Tag

CHAPTER 6
Selecting and Caring for a New Orchid

CHAPTER 7
What Do I Do Now That My Orchid
is Done Blooming?

CHAPTER 3
KNOW YOUR PLANT:
THE NATIVE HABITAT & THE GROWTH HABIT

In all of the gardening classes, seminars, and workshops I teach, from vegetable gardening to basic landscape design, from container gardening to orchids, I always say, "KNOW YOUR PLANT."

Different types of plants thrive in different types of environments and climates. Some like lots of light; some resent lots of light. Some like it wet; some like it dry. Orchids are no different; with almost 1000 genera, orchids as a group are truly as diverse as the entire plant kingdom itself.

To know your plant, local sources of reputable information are always best, e.g. your local gardening club or your favorite garden center. Use caution when using the Internet for plant information. For example, an informed gardener in southern California might post on the Internet how he got his *Cymbidium* orchid to rebloom. If you happen to live in northern Ontario, what he did may not work for you.

I like to impress upon orchid enthusiasts, and all gardeners, the need to understand two lesser emphasized notions that will really help you get to know your orchid (or any plant): ask (1) what is the ***native habitat*** of the plant, or *where does it grow?* i.e. where is it found in nature? (2) what is the ***growth habit*** of the plant, or *how does it grow?* i.e. what does the plant do over the course of one year? Putting these two notions together, I will firmly assert (again) that:

> **The goal for any type of gardening**
> **is to reproduce the *native habitat* of your plant**
> **to get the desired *growth habit* for that plant...**
> **...while having lots of fun.**

THE NATIVE HABITAT OF ORCHIDS

To truly know a particular orchid, you'll want to *know where that orchid is found in nature.* Does the orchid grow on trees in open areas that receive lots of light? Does the orchid grow on rock outcroppings at high elevations in cloud forests? Find out what your orchid experiences growing in its native habitat (e.g. amount of light, rainfall, humidity, temperature range) and how the environment changes during the course of the year. In tropical regions, seasons are distinguished by precipitation and to a lesser extent temperature. In temperate regions, seasons are marked predominantly by the change in temperature and day length.

Two very different environments in Costa Rica within a hundred meters of each other: (left) sunny, open and breezy, warm, humid; (right) shady, cooler, even more humid.

During the European orchid craze of the 1700s (see Chapter 9 The Origin of the Orchid Myth), the lack of knowledge about the native habitats of these newly discovered treasures is precisely why Europeans initially failed to successfully grow orchids. Now we understand the native habitats of orchids all around the world. The hard work has already been done for us.

Here are four attributes of most orchids' native habitats that will greatly assist you in understanding what orchids experience in nature. These environmental attributes give us clues about what to provide for our orchids so they rebloom. This is what we've learned over the past 300 years or so:

(1) The orchids we are talking about in this book are native to tropical regions of the world where the *humidity is significantly greater* than found inside heated or air-conditioned homes.

Yes, there are orchids native to some of the coldest places on the planet. The orchids we are talking about are tropical to subtropical in origin. The humidity found in these tropical climates tends to be higher than that found inside most heated and/or air-conditioned homes. Therefore, we must provide supplemental humidity for our orchids indoors (for most climates), and usually, but not always, outdoors too (for many climates). That's pretty easy to do (see the section in Chapter 2 on "Water, Fertilizer, and Humidity").

(2) In their native habitats, different types of orchids experience *different levels of light*. Some grow in full sun, some grow in lots of shade, and some grow in a combination of sun and shade.

We know now that some orchids prefer direct sun while some require lower light, depending on an orchid's adaptation to light in its specific native habitat. For instance, in the wild, a *Cattleya* orchid may be found growing on the trunk of a tree receiving quite a bit of sun. However, a *Masdevallia* orchid would be found at very high elevations in cool cloud forests bathed in mist, receiving very little direct sun.

We must know whether our orchid likes lots of light, lots of shade, or something in between. Again, pretty easy (see Chapter 2 and Chapter 4).

(3) In the tropics, some orchids are native to low elevations, while some orchids are native to very high elevations, and yet others are native to intermediate elevations.

All other things being equal, the higher one goes in elevation, the cooler the temperatures, especially at night. Some orchids that are native to higher elevations (e.g. *Miltoniopsis*) suffer greatly when temperatures exceed 80F / 27C. Many of the orchids that grow at lower elevations (e.g. *Phalaenopsis*, *Vanda*) rarely experience temperatures under 55-60F / 12-15C. Therefore, they tend to dislike temperatures under 55-60F / 12-15C; again pretty simple.

Many *Cymbidiums* are native to higher elevations. Therefore, to rebloom, they need a decrease in temperature at night, and during fall and winter, so they know what time of year it is. *Cymbidiums* rarely rebloom as year round houseplants, because (1) the temperature remains relatively constant, and they do not "know" what time of year it is, and/or (2) they simply don't receive enough light. As long as temperatures allow, everyone in all climates should grow their *Cymbidiums* outdoors for best reblooming.

You must know what range of temperatures your orchids prefer (see

Chapter 4), AND provide that temperature range for them. Not all homes and outdoor spaces will have temperature ranges suitable for all types of orchids. Therefore, it's best to select orchids that will prefer the range of temperatures normally found inside your home or outdoor environment. Once again, pretty easy (see the section in Chapter 2 on "Temperature").

And the last piece to the puzzle.....THE BIG ONE!

(4) None of the orchids mentioned in this book grow in soil. Most are *epiphytes*; that is, they grow on or in trees!

Many of the orchids described in this book are *epiphytes*, meaning they grow on other plants. Grow on other plants!?! Yes!! The epiphytic character of orchids is one of the most important ideas for understanding proper care. Orchids grow in trees, because that is their naturally adapted location to grow in nature. They are not parasites taking energy from the tree; they just sit there in the tree. It is quite common to see orchids and other plants growing on trees while on vacation in Hawaii, for instance.

This lack of knowledge about the epiphytic character of orchids is the main reason there is the myth, that endures still today, that orchids are difficult to grow. The first attempts to cultivate orchids in Europe several hundred years ago were plagued with failure because nobody knew orchids that were epiphytes and grew in trees. Once the epiphytic character of orchids was properly understood and replicated in cultivation, great strides were made successfully growing and reblooming orchid plants (see Chapter 9 The Origin of the Orchid Myth).

Living in a tree, orchids must have adaptations that enable them to survive dry periods. They will never experience "soggy soil."

Many orchids live in trees, not in soil.

Therefore, they will likely not have adaptations to survive in constantly wet conditions. Some orchids actually grow on rocks and are called lithophytes. "Semi-terrestrial" orchids like *Paphiopedilum* and *Cymbidium*, for instance, grow in leaf litter on the ground, but not in "soil" like carrots and cucumbers do. They too, like epiphytic orchids, *require lots of air for their roots.*

Plants growing in trees experience a lot of moving air. Indoors ventilation or moving air becomes very important. Sometimes a small fan is necessary to prevent roots from rotting during the short days of winter and to move hot air in the heat of summer.

Imagine life in a tree...

Despite the fact that the vast majority of orchids are grown in pots, we know how to to help orchids feel like they are growing as epiphytes or semi-terrestrial plants in their native habitat, e.g. using the appropriate pots and potting media, providing supplemental humidity (see Chapter 2).

It is beyond the scope of this book to explain in detail all the native habitats of all different kinds of orchids. However, Chapter 4 describes, in very general terms, the native habitats for the top ten common groups of orchids. Now let's look at *how* orchids grow...their *growth habit.*

THE GROWTH HABIT OF ORCHIDS

The *growth habit* for any plant describes what the plant "does" over the course of one year. Orchids, like other perennial plants, create new leaves and flowers during certain times of the year, depending on the type of orchid. When does it make new leaves? When does it flower? When does it lose its leaves?

It is not immediately obvious which are the youngest and oldest leaves for this large Cymbidium *orchid plant.*

The ability to differentiate which leaves and growths on any plant are the oldest and which are the youngest not only helps you get to know your plant, but gives you a powerful tool to assess the health of any plant, especially orchids. Sometimes it is obvious which leaves are youngest or oldest; sometimes, especially with older, larger plants, it is not so obvious.

It is common once in a while, for instance, for the oldest leaf of most orchids to turn yellow and fall off. However, if the youngest leaves on any plant look damaged, discolored, or disfigured in any way, something is definitely wrong with the plant.

The ability to discern the youngest leaves from the oldest leaves will empower you to answer questions like: Where will the next flower spike emerge? Should I be concerned that this leaf is turning yellow? Where will the next, new leaf or growth come from?

To answer these and other questions, a basic understanding of an orchid's basic pattern of growth, or growth habit, goes a long way. In terms of growth habits, all orchids are considered to be one of two types, either (1) 'Monopodial,' or (2) 'Symbodial.'

Monopodial Orchids

'Monopodial' literally means 'one foot,' [mono = one; pod = foot]. I look at it as *growing in one direction or with one growth. Phalaenopsis* and *Vanda* are common examples of monopodial orchids. They grow in one direction, up. New leaves are produced alternately above the previous leaves on the same growth. The newest leaves are those on the top of the plant, and the oldest leaves are those at the bottom part of the plant. Pretty simple.

Furthermore, the single "growth" or "shoot" for monopodial orchids never matures and ceases to bloom. That is, the same "shoot" continues to rebloom throughout the life of the plant, like some palms, for example (see the section below on "Flowering").

Monopodial growth habit: growing in one direction, up. The oldest leaves are lowest on the plant, while the youngest leaves are topmost.

Sympodial Orchids

Sympodial orchids are distinctly different from monopodial orchids. They grow laterally or outwards, producing new growths that flower one time (some exceptions). 'Symodial' literally means 'foot together' [sym = with, together; pod = foot] or growing, like most garden perennials, having "many feet together," eventually branching in many directions. Flowers are born only on the plant's newest growths (again, some exceptions) just like with most perennial garden plants (e.g. Bearded Iris, Shasta Daisy).

At the base of each growth are "eyes" or dormant growth buds, not unlike the eyes on a potato or dahlia tuber. There may be one or more eyes at the base of each growth from which new growth has the potential to begin.

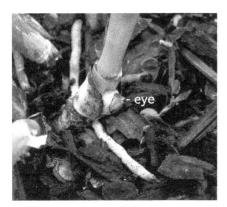 

An "eye" at the base of a Cattleya *pseudobulb from which new growth will emerge.*

As the new shoot emerges, leaves grow and elongate. Some orchids create many leaves per growth (e.g. *Cymbidium*); some grow only one leaf per growth (e.g. some *Cattleya*).

Sympodial growth habit. New leaves emerging on a Cymbidium *orchid (left) and an* Oncidium *orchid (right).*

Most sympodial orchids have "pseudobulbs" or watering storing structures, typically found at the base of each mature growth. In nature, pseudobulbs serve as a water reservoir or water storage organ to assist the youngest parts of the plants during periods when water is scarce. Pseudobulbs range from the size of a pea seed to stem-like "canes" several feet long.

No monopodial orchids have pseudobulbs, and some sympodial orchids lack pseudobulbs (e.g. Lady Slippers, *Tolumnea*). Therefore, generally speaking, I think sympodial orchids have a better ability to recover than monopodial orchids when you water inconsistently or improperly.

Pseudobulbs vary in size and shape: (left) Miltoniopsis - *flat and roundish; (middle)* Dendrobium - *cylindrical to stem-like; (right)* Epidendrum - *slender, stem- or reed-like.*

As new growth matures, the base begins to widen and expand as pseudobulbs mature. For most orchids, flower spikes emerge as or after the new growth or pseudobulb is fully formed; a few orchids (e.g. *Zygopetalum*) bloom *before* the new growth and pseudobulbs are fully mature.

Most orchids in nature "rest" after one cycle of growth and blooming during which time they are growing neither leaves, roots, nor flowers. They rest. Some species (e.g. *Masdevallia*) and hybrids (e.g. in the *Oncidium* Alliance) constantly create new growth and may rebloom a few times a year.

Leaves can remain on some orchids for many years. For other orchids, it is common for the oldest leaves to fall off the oldest pseudobulbs, or "back bulbs." Some deciduous orchids (e.g. some *Dendrobium*) lose all of their leaves every year.

I think sometimes people at first have a hard time understanding the term "sympodial." Besides the fact that most orchids look kinda different from other plants, where the new growth originates and which leaves are oldest or

oldest leaf is turning yellow and will soon fall off

oldest parts
of the plant

youngest parts
of the plant

Sympodial growth habit: Cattleya *orchid growing to the right: the older pseudobulbs are on the left and have lost their leaves; the newest pseudobulbs are on the right.*

youngest is not immediately obvious with sympodial orchids. When you consider that this type of growth habit is basically the same as familiar perennials like Bearded Iris, Daylilies, or Shasta Daisies, it's a lot easier to understand. What confuses the issue is that, unlike these common perennials, orchids have leaves that may persist for many years. This makes it slightly more challenging to distinguish youngest from oldest leaves. The oldest leaves are attached to the oldest growths / pseudobulbs, while the youngest leaves are attached to the youngest growths / pseudobulbs.

Flowering

Most orchids in nature (and almost all plants) bloom during a specific time of the year, typically corresponding with temperature, precipitation or lack of it, and the presence of their native pollinator (e.g. bees, birds, beetles). Many orchids flower in their native habitat during the dry season when native pollinators are more active. How an orchid actually creates flowers and reblooms depends on the growth habit of that orchid. You will understand your orchid plant better when you understand where new flower spikes emerge.

Monopodial Orchids

The flower spikes (and roots) on a monopodial orchid emerge from the leaf axils, the space where the leaf joins the main axis of the plant. For monopodial orchids, reblooming occurs in various places on the same growth throughout the life of the plant, unlike most sympodial orchids.

Emerging new roots and a flower spike on a Phalaenopsis *orchid.*

Sympodial Orchids

Like monopodial orchids, the flowers spikes of sympodial orchids emerge from leaf axils on new growths (some exceptions). However, unlike monopodial orchids, there are many different "types" of leaf axils from which spikes will emerge, depending on the type of orchid.

Some orchids will create flower spikes or "peduncles" in leaf axils on the top of new pseudobulbs (e.g. *Encyclia, Cattleya*); some bloom in leaf axils or at "nodes" on the sides of pseudobulbs (e.g. *Dendrobium*); many orchids create flower spikes in leaf axils at the base of pseudobulbs (e.g. *Miltoniopsis, Cymbidium*).

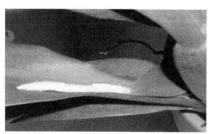

New flower spike emerging in a leaf axil on a sympodial orchid.

Putting it another way and in the most general terms, monopodial orchids can depend on the same growth to rebloom; sympodial orchids, however, must create new growths to rebloom. Of course, there are exceptions.

So What Makes an Orchid, an Orchid?!

It's typically the elegant, distinguished yet sometimes bizarre flowers that tell us we're looking at an orchid. But you might say, "Other plants are epiphytes, and other plants are native to the tropics and have weird flowers. So what makes an orchid an orchid? What does it take for a plant to be considered an orchid?!"

Taxonomists classify or group organisms based on similar characteristics. For plants, the features associated with the flower parts are considered very important when assessing taxonomic relationships. All orchid plants belong in the botanical family 'Orchidaceae.' In very simple terms, plants of the Orchidaceae (i.e. all orchids) have flower parts uniquely arranged in a way unlike all other plants.

All orchid flowers have three sepals (flower bud cover) and three petals, one of which is highly modified and called the "lip." The sepal opposite the lip is the dorsal sepal. Paphiopedilum flowers (right) have two fused lateral sepals, hidden behind the lip.

All orchid flowers have three petals: two lateral petals with the third petal modified into a "lip," the part of the flower that made orchids famous! Orchid flowers also have three sepals: two lateral sepals and a dorsal sepal opposite the lip. When the flower bud is closed, you see the three closed sepals covering the petals inside.

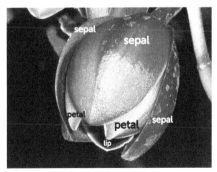

Cymbidium flower bud starting to open. Three sepals cover three petals.

You might say, "Well, lots of flowers have three sepals covering three petals (e.g. Lilies). How are orchids different?!"

OK! What makes orchid flowers distinct from non-orchid flowers is the unique fusion of male and female reproductive parts into a single structure called a "column." The "knob" at the end of the column is called the *operculum*, which covers the pollen sacs underneath. Insects transfer pollen to the gooey stigmatic surface on the underside of the column (not visible in the photo below).

Unique to orchids is the fusion of male and female reproductive parts into a singular structure called a column.

What is a "keiki"?

Keiki is the Hawaiian word for child. Some monopodial (e.g. *Phalaenopsis*) and sympodial orchids (e.g. *Epidendrum*, *Dendrobium*, *Oncidium*) have the potential to produce baby plants or keikis. Many familiar plants have this potential for making baby "plantlets," e.g. spider plant, strawberries, many succulents.

Once keikis have a few roots over 2" long, the keiki may be carefully cut away with a very sharp, sterilized knife or clippers. The keiki is repotted separately and will be an exact copy of the mother plant. It may be anywhere from one to a few years before the keiki blooms.

The presence of a keiki *sometimes* indicates that the plant is unhappy *in its pot* and is trying to propagate itself so that it can live somewhere else. *Phalaenopsis* orchids may create keikis when they have been overwatered, have not been repotted in a long time, or are otherwise unhappy in their pot. *Dendrobium* orchids may produce keikis instead of flower spikes if they do not receive similar water and temperatures found in their native habitat year round.

The term "keiki" refers to a baby plant that grows on flowers spikes and pseudobulbs. **Upper left:** Phalaenopsis *keiki growing on a flower spike.* **Upper right:** Epidendrum *keiki growing on a flower spike.* **Below:** Dendrobium *keiki growing on a pseudobulb.*

COMMON QUESTIONS & ANSWERS
ABOUT HOW TO "KNOW YOUR PLANT"

Q: What does an orchid's native habitat refer to?

A: A plant's native habitat refers to the environment or region where it would be found growing wild, "out there in nature," before humans moved them all over the place.

Q: Why is it important to know something about the native habitat of my orchid(s)?

A: In all of our gardening endeavors, what we are really trying to do is to reproduce the native habitat of our plants. The environmental conditions that an orchid experiences in its native habitat give us clues about how to take care of that particular orchid (e.g. when to water less, how much light is needed). That is, we try to make our plant feel like it is living in its native habitat, which also happens to be the conditions required for it to rebloom!! Know your plant.

Q: What does the growth habit of an orchid refer to?

A: The growth habit of a plant describes how a plant grows, or what the plant does over the course of one year. For instance, the growth habit describes, among other things: When does the plant make new leaves? When does the plant flower? Does the plant lose its leaves? See the next question.

Q: Why is it important to understand the *growth habit* of my orchid(s)?

A: Understanding the growth habit of your orchid, or any plant, helps you understand when and where the plant will be making new leaves, when it should be flowering, when it rests or experiences dormancy, and more. Knowing this enables you to determine the best time to repot your orchids or what time of year to water more / less often, for instance.

By understanding the growth habit of your orchid, you will be able to differentiate between the youngest and oldest leaves on a plant. Knowing which leaves are youngest or oldest gives you a powerful tool to assess the overall health of your orchid...and any plant.

Q: Why are orchids considered difficult to grow?

A: The lack of understanding about the native habitat of orchids historically, and to this day, is the main reason orchids are considered difficult to grow.

The first orchids brought back to Europe in the 1700s quickly perished, because little was known about their native habitat in the tropics. Once the epiphytic nature and knowledge of varying temperature and light requirements were understood, orchids began to thrive and rebloom (see Chapter 9 The Origin of the Orchid Myth).

Still to this day many people do not realize that most orchids are epiphytes, that they live in trees. Orchids commonly suffer when cared for like "regular" houseplants. The most common houseplants like peace lily, philodendron, spider plant, dracaena, etc. are not epiphytes. They require more frequent waterings and a totally different potting media than most orchids. As a result, and as stated above in Chapter 2, overwatering remains to this day the most common reason orchids die.

Q: What is a pseudobulb, and what is its function?
A: A pseudobulb is a water holding structure unique to *certain types* of sympodial orchids. Its function is to store water and supply it to the "front" or youngest, actively growing part of the plant when water is lacking. A pseudobulb is an adaptation that prevents orchids from drying out "up there in the tree." The pseudobulb becomes a lifesaver during extended dry periods, or when you forget to water...jus' sayin.'

Q: What is the difference between monopodial and sympodial orchids?
A: The terms refer to the two different ways orchids grow. **Monopodial orchids** (e.g. *Phalaenopsis, Vanda*) grow predominantly in one direction, up. They rely on one main growth or shoot to rebloom throughout their lives, like some palm trees. **Sympodial orchids** (e.g. *Cattleya, Paphiopedilum, Oncidium*) grow new growths or shoots, much like common perennials. Unlike monopodial orchids, most sympodial orchids rely on the production of new growths to rebloom; there are some exceptions, e.g. *Dendrobium*.

Q: Why is it important to know the differences between monopodial and sympodial orchids?
A: Understanding your orchid's growth habit will help you to: differentiate between the youngest and oldest leaves on plants, assess the overall health of your plant, properly repot your orchid when the time is right (see Chapter 2), among other things.

Q: What are some examples of common monopodial orchids?

A: *Phalaenopsis*, *Vanda*, and their hybrids, to name a few.

Q: What are some examples of common sympodial orchids that grow pseudobulbs?

A: *Oncidium, Odontoglossum, Cymbidium, Dendrobium, Miltonia, Brassia, Zygopetalum*, and many, many more.

Q: What are some examples of sympodial orchids that lack pseudobulbs?

A: *Dracula, Masdevallia, Paphiopedilum, Phragmipedium, Tolumnea.*

Q: What are some examples of monopodial orchids with pseudobulbs?

A: There are no monopodial orchids with pseudobulbs.

Q: How do I know which leaves, growths, and pseudobulbs are the youngest and oldest?

A: Know your plant! For orchids with a monopodial growth habit, the oldest leaves are the bottommost leaves on the plant, and the youngest leaves are topmost on the plant.

To determine the oldest part of a sympodial orchid, look for a "back bulb," a pseudobulb lacking leaves. On a mature plant with many pseudobulbs, you'll often find a few pseudobulbs lacking leaves; this is the oldest part of the plant. At least some of the newest, youngest leaves and growth will be growing closest to the edge of the pot.

If you are having difficulty determining which leaves are youngest vs. oldest, take your orchid to an independent nursery or orchid specialist and have them show you. *Trust me, it's really important you figure this one out.*

Q: Why is it important to be able to distinguish between the oldest and the youngest leaves?

A: Being able to differentiate between the youngest versus oldest leaves gives you a powerful tool to assess the health of any plant, especially orchids. For instance, it is common for most plants, including orchids, to shed their oldest leaf once in a while. That is, the oldest leaf on almost any plant will at some point turn yellow and fall off. However, if the youngest leaf looks damaged, disfigured or discolored in any way, you know something is definitely wrong with your plant (see the section in Chapter 10 on "Problems with Leaves").

Q: Why is my orchid making this little baby plant on the flower spike?
A: Some orchids have the potential to create a baby plantlet (keiki) on flowers spikes (e.g. *Phalaenopsis, Epidendrum*) or on pseudobulbs (e.g. *Dendrobium, Oncidium*). An orchid sometimes creates a keiki when it is unhappy in its pot and is trying to grow elsewhere. *Phalaenopsis* can create keikis when they have been overwatered, have not been repotted in a long time, or are otherwise unhappy in the pot. Some *Dendrobium* orchids may produce keikis instead of flower spikes if they receive improper winter temperatures or if kept constantly wet without the watering rest they need once new growth matures.

Q: Why are the roots of my orchid growing up and out of the pot?
A: First, most orchids we are talking about are epiphytes. For life in a tree, an orchid grows roots, both to grab moisture and to anchor itself in the tree in which it is growing. When potted, some of these roots will naturally point up and not make it down in the pot.

Second, sometimes orchids grow roots outside the pot when the plant is unhappy inside the pot. Often when roots are rotting in the pot, usually from overwatering, the plant figures it's better to grow roots outside and on top of the pot.

If you see an abundance of roots outside the pot, take the plant out of the pot and inspect the roots. If almost all of the roots in the pot are dead, repotting will be necessary, sometimes into a smaller pot. If most or all of the roots in the pot look healthy and the potting media looks bad, repot it at the appropriate time (see the section in Chapter 2 on "Repotting").

CHAPTER 4
THE TOP 10
COMMON GROUPS OF ORCHIDS

Here are what I call The Top 10 Common Groups of Orchids. Almost all orchids found at nurseries, florists, garden shops, and grocery stores will belong to one of these ten groups. This chapter presents the basic information you will need for reblooming each group.

It's hard to be both thorough and precise for such diverse genera as *Dendrobium* or the immense *Oncidium* Alliance. More can definitely be said, and exceptions to my highly generalized guidelines abound. I've distilled the most pertinent information you will need for your particular Top 10 orchid to rebloom. If your orchid is not in one of the Top 10 groups, this chapter shows you what types of relevant reblooming information you need to have.

KNOW YOUR PLANT describes the growth habit, native habitat, and environmental requirements for reblooming. "Check It Out" gives fantastic, fun facts about each group.

REBLOOMING ORCHIDS gives
1) Helpful hints for reblooming
2) What to do when your orchids has finished blooming
3) Challenges to reblooming.

Orange boxes summarize reblooming requirements for each group.

This chapter and this book, or any book for that matter, will likely not enable you to definitively identify every orchid. Determining which specific hybrid or species your orchid is may not be possible until flowers are present.

However, you can often determine which of the Top 10 groups your orchid belongs to by observing the size and shape of leaves and pseudobulbs if present. Under "Growth Habit," I describe the leaves and pseudobulbs in a way that distinguishes that group from the other nine groups.

THE *CATTLEYA* ALLIANCE
The Corsage Orchids

Cattleyas *or the "Corsage Orchids" are iconic in the orchid world!*

KNOW YOUR PLANT!

Growth Habit: Sympodial; one to a few thick, stiff leaves atop cylindrical-shaped pseudobulbs; some have egg-shaped to teardrop-shaped pseudobulbs and thinner, strap-like leaves. Highly variable in shape and size.

Flowering Habit: Blooms emerge from the top of mature pseudobulbs, sometimes months after the pseudobulb has fully formed.

Native Habitat: Epiphytes, some lithophytes; large native range from mid to high elevations in tropical forests in Central and South America.

Light: Lots of light for most.

Watering: Water more frequently when growing leaves; water much less often when not growing leaves.

Temperature: Intermediate temperatures for most, cool for some. Avoid excessive heat.

Potting Media: Medium- to fine-grade for most, depending on the type; semi-terrestrial mix for reed-stem *Epidendrums.*

Generally Speaking

The *Cattleya* Alliance is an interbreeding group of genera, including: *Brassavola, Cattleya, Encyclia, Epidendrum, Guarianthe, Laelia, Rhyncholaelia, Sophronitis,* and more. Keeping track of the numerous intergeneric hybrids (i.e. hybrids between different genera) is not a small task. See Chapter 5 The Orchid Identification Tag regarding naming hybrids.

Cattleyas grow primarily as epiphytes, native to mid to high elevations in South America. They typically require lots of light and a good drop in temperature at night.

Flowers of the Cattleya *Alliance display an amazing array of colors and fragrances!!*

Check It Out!

It was, in part, the *Cattleya* orchid with its large flamboyant flowers that helped start the orchid craze long ago.

Some orchids in the *Cattleya* Alliance grow only one leaf per growth!

Some members of the genera *Epidendrum* and *Prosthechea* (formerly *Encyclia*) have the potential to rebloom on the same flower spike!

Epidendrum orchids are grouped into two kinds: (1) pseudobulb types, which appear and grow like other members of the *Cattleya* Alliance, and (2) the "reed-stem" *Epidendrums* which make thin, stem-like pseudobulbs. Reed-stem *Epidendrums* are very tough and bloom year round as landscaping ornamentals in appropriate climates.

REBLOOMING *CATTLEYA* ORCHIDS

Helpful Hints for Reblooming

Grow *Cattleyas* and their relatives outdoors whenever possible, as long as it's not too hot in the summer nor too cold in the winter. Outdoors they will receive better light, excellent ventilation, and cooler night temperatures. Be sure to water less often when the plant is flowering or resting, i.e. not growing leaves. Repot as new growth emerges.

Be sure to provide the proper potting media. Seedlings and young plants will prefer fine bark while most older plants prefer medium bark. Give reed-stem *Epidendrums* semi-terrestrial mix similar to that used for *Cymbidium* and Lady Slipper orchids - know your plant! For many *Cattleya* orchids and their relatives, it is best to repot just as new roots and shoots emerge.

Be patient! Some will bloom right after new growth matures while the sheath covering the bud is still fresh and green. Others bloom many months after the new growth matures.

The cockleshell orchid (Prosthechea cochleata) *has long-blooming, unusually shaped flowers. It is one of the easiest* Cattleya *Alliance orchids to rebloom as a houseplant.*

When Finished Blooming

For most orchids in this group, cut off the spent bloom spike as far down as you can without hurting the plant. After blooming, provide lots of light and water less frequently *unless or until* new growth is emerging.

A couple of exceptions are *Encyclia* (some now called *Prosthechea*) and the "reed-stem" *Epidendrums*. When happy, they continue to rebloom off the end of the existing flower spike.

Challenges to Reblooming

Indoors, the most common challenge is providing enough light for reblooming. Outdoors, snails and slugs love *Cattleya* buds and flowers.

Epidendrum orchids have the potential to bloom all year long. In the appropriate climates, they make excellent landscaping plants.

TO REBLOOM, *CATTLEYA* ORCHIDS REQUIRE:
Lots of light, all year long.
Less water when not growing leaves.
A nice drop in the evening temperature.
Proper grade potting media.
Repotting only when new roots / growth begins.

CYMBIDIUM
Magnificent and Stately

Cymbidiums grow large, long-lasting flowers on thick, sturdy spikes; they make excellent year round outdoor container plants in cool but frost-free regions.

KNOW YOUR PLANT!

Growth Habit: Sympodial. Tough, long, strap-like leaves 12-48" long and 1/2-2" wide with egg-shaped pseudobulbs ranging in size from 1-5" tall.

Flowering Habit: Blooms emerge from leaf axils at the base of new growth after pseudobulbs mature, from late fall into spring, depending on the type.

Native Habitat: Mainly semi-terrestrial, a few epiphytes and lithophytes. Mid to high elevations in tropical SE Asia, from India to Japan to Australia.

Light: Plenty of light without heat.

Watering: Water liberally, and fertilize during spring and summer when growing leaves. Water far less often when blooming; sometimes only a couple of times per month during winter.

Temperature: Cool; avoid temperatures over 80-85F / 27-30C. Must receive cool nights under 50-55F / 10-13C to rebloom.

Potting Media: "Semi-terrestrial" orchid mix or chunky coconut fiber. With regular and timely repotting, *Cymbidiums* can grow into enormous specimens within several years.

Generally Speaking

Cymbidiums are cool-growing, semi-terrestrial orchids that bloom mainly during winter and spring. "Standard" varieties have leaves over 3 feet long with large, 3-5" flowers eventually becoming spectacular specimen plants. "Miniatures" and newer hybrids have leaves from 12-30" long and smaller flowers.

Bold, long-lasting flowers have intricate lip markings and intense colorations.

Cymbidium *orchids can grow into large specimen plants = you will need space.*

Water more often once new growth begins and the plant is growing leaves.

Water less often when in bloom.

Check it Out!

Outdoors in frost-free climates, *Cymbidium* orchids make excellent year round container plants. The west coast of North America is one of the best locations in the world to grow *Cymbidium* orchids.

Though not grown for fragrance, *Cymbidium* orchids bloom in a wide range of colors. They make excellent long-lasting cut flowers on large flower spikes from 1-4 feet long.

Confucius' writings 2500 years ago contain the oldest reference to orchids, likely referring to *Cymbidium goeringii*, which tolerates snow.

REBLOOMING *CYMBIDIUM* ORCHIDS

Helpful Hints for Reblooming

Grow outdoors whenever frost-free temperatures allow! They require cool fall and winter nights close to or under 50F / 10C to form flower buds.

Be sure to water regularly when growing leaves, and water much less frequently when in spike or bloom. When blooming and brought indoors, keep as cool as possible, *especially at night*. Flowers last much longer when plants are kept cool and watered less often.

Avoid shallow pots; use proportionately deeper pots to accommodate their vigorous root system; use "semi-terrestrial" orchid media or orchid mix.

Use sturdy, strong stakes to stabilize flower spikes *as they emerge*. The flower spikes are very brittle, and once longer than 12," easily snap when handled.

Cymbidiums *will not rebloom as year round houseplants. Grow outdoors whenever possible in a cool but frost-free location.*

When Finished Blooming

Cut off the spent bloom spike down as far as you can without hurting the plant.

Challenges to Reblooming

Cymbidium orchids rarely rebloom indoors as houseplants, because light is lacking and/or the night temperatures are not low enough. Keep cool. Many will not perform well in climates with hot summer days and/or nights.

If suddenly moved from cold conditions to warm indoor conditions, or *if they are overwatered*, the flowers will not last as long and buds can fall off prematurely (see the section in Chapter 10 on "Bud Blast").

Insufficient water when leaves are growing inhibits reblooming. Water consistently and more often when leaves are growing during summer.

Be careful not to bump the brittle flower spikes as they emerge; if they break, that's it...

Big plants; big flowers; lotsa colors; long bloom time!!

TO REBLOOM, *CYMBIDIUM* ORCHIDS REQUIRE:
Lots of light with *cool temperatures* - not hot!
Regular water when growing leaves,
Less water when flowering or not growing leaves.
Outdoors whenever possible; avoid frosts or excessive heat.
Semi-terrestrial grade potting media; avoid shallow pots.

DENDROBIUM
The Bamboo Orchid

The immense genus Dendrobium! *Species and hybrids are highly variable in size, shape, color, and fragrance of flowers. Plants range from just a few inches to many feet tall.*

KNOW YOUR PLANT!

Growth Habit: Sympodial; short, strap-like leaves grow from nodes and/or tops of stem-shaped or cane-like pseudobulbs. Huge variety in size and shape of plants from just a few inches to several feet tall!

Flowering Habit: Individual flower spikes or flowers emerge from top or sides of mature pseudobulbs; some will rebloom on the same pseudobulb.

Native Habitat: Epiphytes from tropical and sub-tropical SE Asia, the South Pacific, Australia, and New Zealand.

Light: Most need lots of light without excessive heat.

Watering: Watering infrequently during winter and when not growing leaves is very important for reblooming.

Temperature: Warm to cool; widely ranging depending on the type.

Potting Media: Most require medium-grade potting media; some require a fine-grade potting media.

You will find various ways of grouping or classifying *Dendrobium* orchids. I like the four groups outlined by Cullina (2004) based not on taxonomy, but based on environmental conditions found in their native habitats (i.e. what environmental conditions they require to rebloom).

(1) Winter deciduous or "*nobile*" type, referring to *Dendrobium nobile*
Intermediate temperatures most of the year.
During winter, provide cool nights under 60F / 15C, and less water.
Flowering often occurs after leaves fall off.

(2) Intermediate- to cool-growing, evergreen type
Intermediate temperatures most of the year.
Provide cool temperatures and much less water during winter.
Includes the popular and fragrant *D. kingianum.*
Flowering occurs when pseudobulbs are mature, leaves remain for years.

(3) Cloud forest type
Require high humidity, regular water, and fine-grade potting media.
Intermediate to cool temperatures.
Typically smaller plants.

(4) Warm, evergreen type
Warm temperatures, never under 55-60F / 13-15C.
Lots of light; grows well indoors in sunny, humid locations.
Medium-grade potting media.
Includes Phalaenanthe, Latouria, and Spatulata types of *Dendrobium.*

'Phalaenanthe'-type Dendrobiums *prefer warm temperatures.*

Generally Speaking

Dendrobium is one of the largest and most diverse of the orchid genera. Species and hybrids vary greatly in their light and temperature requirements. Providing the correct temperatures and less water during winter are the main keys to reblooming *Dendrobium* orchids.

What almost all *Dendrobium* orchids have in common is that they require: lots of light; small pots for exceptional drainage and air for roots; high humidity and good air movement; proper temperatures, especially during Winter; much less water and fertilizer during Winter.

Dendrobium kingianum *retains its leaves for many years; the flowers are fragrant!!*

Yes, not only is this an orchid, it is also in the genus Dendrobium = D. faciferum.

Check it Out!

Both species and hybrids display a marked diversity in flower color, shape, and fragrance. *Dendrobium* bloom in almost every color imaginable, and many are nicely fragrant.

Cane-like pseudobulbs range in size from under an inch to several feet tall. Bloom spikes emerge from the top (e.g. *D. kingianum*) or sides of pseudobulbs (e.g. *D. nobile*). *Dendrobiums* readily form keikis, sometimes as a result of improper temperatures and/or watering *during winter*.

From the bizarre *D. spectabile,* to the orange *D. unicum*, to the very fragrant *D. anosmum*, to the intricate 'Antelope'-types, to the purplish-blue *D. victoria-reginae*, there is sure to be a *Dendrobium* for everyone!

The spectacular 'nobile'-type Dendrobiums *lose their leaves as flowering begins!*

REBLOOMING *DENDROBIUM* ORCHIDS

Helpful Hints for Reblooming

Good light, extra humidity, and air movement all year long are essential for reblooming *Dendrobium* orchids. As with most orchids, water more often when the plant is growing new leaves. Water much less often and do not fertilize during winter.

Use "smallish" pots for two reasons: (1) to provide for exceptional drainage, so the roots receive plenty of air, and (2) the narrow, vertical shape of the growths and pseudobulbs means *Dendrobium* orchids won't fill their pots as fast as other orchids like Cymbidium.

Know which kind of *Dendrobium* you have so that you provide proper temperatures during the winter rest. Use the correct grade of potting media for your particular *Dendrobium* orchid.

 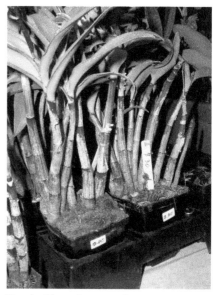

The very unusual, Dendrobium unicum.   Dendrobiums *love small pots.*

When Finished Blooming

Cut off spent flower spikes without damaging leaves or pseudobulbs. *D. nobile*-type orchids bloom on very short spikes from nodes on the sides of pseudobulbs; they have no real flower spike (peduncle) to remove. Water much less frequently after blooming and when no leaves are growing, especially during winter.

Challenges to Reblooming

There are two main obstacles to reblooming for the would be *Dendrobium* enthusiast, both resulting from not knowing that (1) there are four main types of *Dendrobium* orchids, each requiring slightly different environmental conditions, and that (2) during winter *Dendrobium* orchids require proper temperatures and much less water and fertilizer.

Indoors, the main challenge is providing enough light and humidity year round, especially during winter when your heater is on.

A red edge along the leaf margin of some types indicates the plant is receiving the maximum amount of light (and heat) the plant will tolerate.

Dendrobium *Hsinying Chrysopense*

Dendrobium victoria-reginae, *yes, blue!*

Dendrobium spectabile. *Wow!!! That's a flower?!*

The appropriately named Dendrobium pendulum *with hanging pseudobulbs.*

TO REBLOOM, *DENDROBIUM* ORCHIDS REQUIRE:
A lot of light all year long.
Proper temperature and much less water during winter.
Good humidity and air movement.
"Smallish" pots and the correct grade of potting media.

MASDEVALLIA / DRACULA
Cloud Forest Novelties

Masdevallia *and* Dracula *orchids are small plants with intricate flower markings.*

KNOW YOUR PLANT!

Growth Habit: Sympodial, lacking pseudobulbs. Thick, flexible strap-like leaves, wider at the top and narrower at the base, grow year round.

Flowering Habit: Flower spikes emerge from the base of new mature leaves; some rebloom on the same flower spike. *Dracula* orchids have pendulous flower spikes that emerge from the bottom or sides of slatted hanging baskets.

Native Habitat: Epiphytes, lithophytes, or semi-terrestrial at high elevations in cloud forests in Central and South America.

Light: Bright but indirect light; shade from hot sun.

Watering: Maintain consistently moist potting media; watering frequency depends more on temperature than on growth habit or time of year.

Temperature: Cool with high humidity; avoid temperatures over 80F / 27C.

Potting Media: Fine-grade potting media.

Generally Speaking

Masdevallia, and their close relatives *Dracula*, are native to high elevations in the cool, humid, cloud forests of South America. They are easy to grow and rebloom (even in artificial light) when given indirect light, cool, humid conditions, and good air movement. Many are "free-blooming," continuing to flower as long as the plant is growing leaves. They do not require a watering rest period and should never be allowed to dry out completely.

What you are mainly looking at in a Masdevallia *flower are not the three petals, but* **the three sepals!** *The three petals are actually quite small in the center of the flower.*

Check It Out!

What you see when you look at a *Masdevallia* or *Dracula* flower are actually the three "sepals," not the three "petals" of the flower (see Chapter 3); the petals are very small and reduced in size in the center of the flower. The decorative and delicate tails on the end of the sepals give each kind of *Masdevallia* and *Dracula* its own unique character.

The genus *Dracula* was formerly included within the genus *Masdevallia*; both require the same basic care. One curious difference is that *Dracula* orchids are typically grown in slatted hanging pots so that pendulous flower spikes can emerge out of the bottom or sides of the pot!

Some *Dracula* orchid flowers are larger than the entire plant!

REBLOOMING *MASDEVALLIAS* and *DRACULAS*

Helpful Hints for Reblooming

Provide cool temperatures with high humidity and good air movement. Most *Masdevallia / Dracula* orchids do not require a watering rest, because they grow and bloom year round. This lack of a rest reflects their native habitat where environmental conditions remain relatively consistent throughout the year. Once a month water the pot thoroughly without fertilizer to flush excess salts.

Almost all *Dracula* and some *Masdevallia* require slatted hanging baskets so that their pendulous (hanging) flower spikes can emerge from the bottom or side of the pot. Use fine-grade potting media.

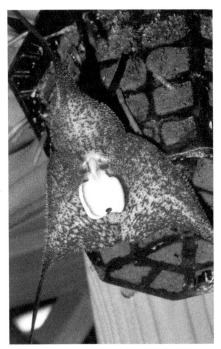

Dracula *orchids require slatted baskets so that the pendulous or hanging flower spike can emerge through the bottom or side of the pot. Here is* Dracula bella.

When Finished Blooming

As usual, know your plant! Some *Masdevallia,* like the white flowering *M. tovarensis*, has the ability to rebloom on the same flower spike the following year! Otherwise, when blooms are spent, simply cut off the flower spike as far back as you can without hurting the plant.

Challenges to Reblooming

Lack of humidity, especially in heated homes during winter months, is the biggest challenge to reblooming. Use a humidity tray. Misting is recommended, but only in well-ventilated environments.

Masdevallia and *Dracula* dislike missed waterings and temperatures over 80F / 27C. As mentioned above, they grow in fairly exacting, consistent environments in their native habitats.

Problems, besides not reblooming, occur when conditions stray away from those found in their native habitat. For instance, brown or black leaf tips can result from: lack of water and/or humidity, excessive salts in water, or high temperatures.

Masdevallia *and* Dracula *orchids prefer moist, cool, moving air.*

TO REBLOOM, *MASDEVALLIA* & *DRACULA* ORCHIDS REQUIRE:
Cool temperatures.
High humidity and good air movement.
Fine-grade potting media.

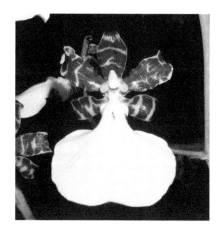

THE *ONCIDIUM* ALLIANCE

The **Oncidium** **Alliance** is perhaps the largest group of interbreeding genera within the entire orchid family. Dozens of species within each genus create the potential for an innumerable array of hybrids with tremendous and spectacular variability in flower color, shape, and fragrance.

This immense group of orchids has a huge native range starting in southern North America, throughout Central America, and most of South America. Within this large, diverse area there are numerous habitats from dry and hot, to cloudy and cool.

As mentioned previously, for your orchid to rebloom, you must reproduce the environmental conditions found in your orchid's native habitat. I have therefore, for your convenience and ease of understanding, separated the *Oncidium* Alliance into two groups (1) cool growers and (2) the warm and intermediate growers.

The "cool-growing" orchids in the *Oncidium* Alliance are native to high elevations. They experience cooler environmental conditions that remain relatively consistent over the course of the year: temperatures fluctuate within a narrower range, and moisture is more consistently available. This type of habitat differs from the habitats of orchids native to lower to middle elevations that prefer warm to intermediate temperatures.

Hybrids are typically more forgiving plants, because they tolerate a wider range of environmental conditions than their parents tolerate. Some hybrids rebloom more frequently, both indoors and outdoors. With all the *Oncidium* hybrids, naming can be bewildering (see Chapter 5); names are constantly changing, and hybrids can result from two to six or more genera.

As mentioned at the beginning of this chapter, without the ID tag, you will not be able to definitively identify your specific hybrid or species of orchid with this book, or any other book. Once you know your orchid is in the *Oncidium* group, you will need to find out its temperature preferences. Without the ID tag or the flowers being present, it's not that easy. Relatively speaking, the thicker the leaf (actual thickness of the leaf, not the width), the more it will tolerate higher temperatures; the thinner and more flexible the leaf, the more it dislikes higher temperatures. If you have a photo of a flower, show it to your local orchid club or society, and ask for assistance determining the specific name.

ONCIDIUM ALLIANCE
Cool temperature growers

**Miltoniopsis, Oncidium (formerly Odontoglossum),
Rhynchostele, Cochlioda, and others**

The Oncidium *Alliance: an amazing array of colors, intricate markings, and fragrances!*

KNOW YOUR PLANT!

Growth Habit: Sympodial; most have thin, narrow, flexible strap-like leaves that grow atop and at the base of flat, oval-shaped pseudobulbs 1" to 3" tall.

Flowering Habit: Flower spikes emerge from leaf axils once pseudobulbs are mature.

Native Habitat: Epiphytes; medium to high elevations in Central and South America.

Light: As much light as possible while maintaining cool temperatures.

Watering: Consistent water, especially when growing leaves; some, especially hybrids, are constantly growing leaves. Water less during coldest time of year.

Temperature: Cool, usually preferring a narrow range of temperatures, optimally between 60-80F / 15-27C.

Potting Media: Fine-grade potting media accommodates their need for fairly consistent moisture throughout the year.

Generally Speaking

These cool-growing, heavily hybridized members of the *Oncidium* Alliance are easy to grow and rebloom as long as their temperature and watering requirements are met: lots of light while avoiding hot sun; narrow range of cool temperatures, often with no watering rest.

Many of these orchids will rebloom under artificial lights. Those native to cloud forests (e.g. *Rhynchostele*) are easy to grow as houseplants because they don't need tons of light; you just need to keep them humid and cool.

Miltoniopsis, or the Pansy Orchids will not rebloom in hot temperatures over 80-85F / 27-30C. Provide cool, humid conditions and more consistent water year round.

Check it Out!

Miltoniopsis should not to be confused with *Miltonia. Miltoniopsis* are native to higher elevations and prefer cooler temperatures than *Miltonia* orchids prefer. They make new growths almost year round and require fairly consistent moisture. Leaves of *Miltoniopsis* normally have a grayish, light-green color.

Some cool-growing *Oncidium* orchids and their hybrids were formerly named in the separate genus *Odontoglossum*. You will likely still encounter this name in your orchid collecting, especially among hybrids.

REBLOOMING Cool-Growing *ONCIDIUM* ORCHIDS

Helpful Hints for Reblooming

Provide more consistent water than for most warm-growing members of the *Oncidium* Alliance. Water regularly when growing leaves. Lots of bright light while maintaining cool temperatures, never > 80F / 27C, is absolutely essential for reblooming. Most will rebloom under artificial light.

Miltoniopsis require frequent repotting, because their almost constant growth rapidly fills the pot. On the other hand, the roots of the cool-growing *Oncidiums* formerly named *Odontoglossum* are susceptible to rot. They benefit from remaining in smaller pots with more frequent waterings so that roots have easy access to air.

Rossioglossum grande, *or the clown orchid, has flowers up to 6" across!!!*

When Finished Blooming

Cut off the spent flower spike as far back as your can without hurting the plant; leave a little stump of the spike so you can prove to your friends that your orchid did actually rebloom!

Challenges to Reblooming

The two biggest challenges to reblooming are providing consistent moisture and humidity, and maintaining temperatures in the ideal range, 60-80F / 15-27C. Providing humid, moving air can be a big challenge in heated homes. Indoors, do not mist to avoid water sitting in the folds of the leaves. Pseudobulbs rapidly shrivel with inconsistent water or less than ideal humidity. These orchids can be difficult to rebloom outdoors in hot summer climates.

Miltoniopsis orchids, and their hybrids, quickly grow to fill their pots and need regular repotting. Failure to repot often results in symptoms of underwatering, which can result in "pleated" leaves (see the section in Chapter 10 on "Problems With Leaves") and failure to rebloom.

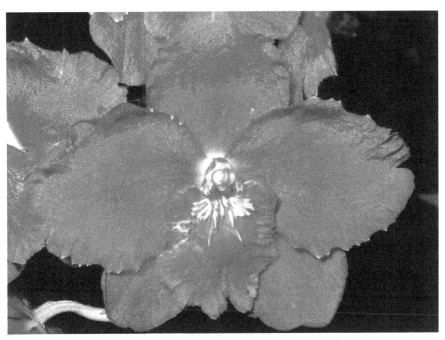

Oncidium *Alliance orchids with predominanatly red flowers require cool temperaures because of the cool-growing genus* Cochlioda *in their parentange.*

TO REBLOOM, COOL-GROWING *ONCIDIUM* ORCHIDS REQUIRE:
As much light as possible while maintaining cool temperatures.
High humidity and good air movement.
Fine-grade potting media and more consistent waterings.
Repotting before plants overgrow pots.

ONCIDIUM ALLIANCE
Intermediate to Warm Growers
Brassia, Miltonia, Oncidium and others

The intermediate and warm growers are just as spectacular as the cool growers.

KNOW YOUR PLANT!

Growth Habit: Sympodial; most have thin, narrow, flexible strap-like leaves that grow atop and at the base of flat, oval-shaped pseudobulbs, ranging in size from 1" to over 6" tall; some (e.g. *Tolumnea*) lack pseudobulbs.

Flowering Habit: For most, flower spikes emerge from leaf axils on new, mature pseudobulbs; some rebloom on the same flower spike!

Native Habitat: Mainly epiphytes; huge range from southern North America to Central America to southern South America, from open sunny habitats (e.g. some *Oncidium*), to humid, part-shade environments (e.g. *Miltonia*).

Light: Typically lots of light; some less than others. Generally, the thicker the leaf, the more sun and higher temperatures they require or tolerate.

Watering: Water more frequently when growing leaves and less frequently when not growing leaves.

Temperature: Widely ranging, from intermediate to warm temperatures.

Potting Media: Medium- to fine-grade depending on the type.

Generally Speaking

Warm- and intermediate-growing members of the *Oncidium* Alliance require lots of sun and good humidity to rebloom. The thicker the leaf, the more sun they need. *Miltonia* orchids dislike hot sun. Know your genus!

The many different species in the *Oncidium* Alliance typically flower during a specific time of the year. Some hybrids, however, constantly create new growths and can rebloom 2-3 times over one year. Hybridizing warm growers with cool growers often results in offspring tolerant of a wide range of temperatures, which is great for the orchid hobbyist!

The popular hybrid, Oncidium *Sharry Baby 'Sweet Fragrance,' has tantalizing chocolate / vanilla scented flowers and reblooms two to three times each year.*

Tolumnea, *formerly "equitant"* Oncidium, *are small plants, lacking pseudobulbs, with succulent, fan-shaped leaves. They can rebloom on the same flower spike!*

Check it Out!

Many *Oncidium* species (e.g. *O. ornithorhynchum*) and hybrids (e.g. O. Sharry Baby 'Sweet Fragrance') are famously fragrant. *Brassia* orchids have slender spider-shaped flowers, some over 12" tall.

Tolumnea, formerly called "equitant *Oncidium*," are a unique group of small plants with succulent, fan-shaped (equitant) leaves and *no pseudobulbs. Tolumneas* rebloom on the original flower spike, so do not cut it off. They like it warm with exceptional drainage, and never under 60F / 15C.

Also within the *Oncidium* Alliance is the unusual and alien-like *Psychopsis papilio* (formerly *Oncidium papilio*) that reblooms on flower spikes from many years past!

Some members of the *Oncidium* Alliance can form keikis on top of pseudobulbs.

REBLOOMING Intermediate- and Warm-Growing *ONCIDIUM* ORCHIDS

Helpful Hints for Reblooming

Plenty of light and humidity are absolutely essential to reblooming. Generally, the thicker the leaf the more sun and heat they will tolerate; avoid excessive heat over 90F / 32C. *Miltonia* and others with thinner leaves dislike hot sun greater than 80-85F / 27-30C.

When Finished Blooming

Know your plant! Some will rebloom on the same flower spike (e.g. *Tolumnea*), sometimes years later (e.g. *Psychopsis*). Otherwise, as usual, cut off the spent flower spike as far back as you can without hurting the plant.

The amazing Butterfly Orchid, Psychopsis papilio, *has huge flowers and reblooms on the same spike.....years later!!!*

Challenges to Reblooming

By far the most common challenge *indoors* is providing enough light year round for *Oncidiums* and their relatives that require a lot of light to rebloom. Otherwise they can be grown outdoors in the same basic conditions as *Cattleyas* while, as usual, avoiding lots of heat.

Providing adequate humidity is often a challenge especially in heated homes during winter. The youngest leaves on new growth will often stick together and not unfold if the air and/or plant is too dry. Furthermore, pseudobulbs quickly shrivel if the humidity is low or waterings are missed.

Some *Oncidium* Alliance hybrids have the potential to create so many new growths each year that they require repotting more frequently than most other orchids. It is very important to repot before the plant starts to grow over the edge of the pot. Failure to do so inhibits reblooming, because new roots hang over the edge of the pot and have a harder time receiving the water they need.

This number of possible hybrid genera makes naming (or re-naming) a challenge as current research helps us better understand taxonomical interrelationships. Know your plant name and see Chapter 5.

The hybrids involving Brassia *have spectacular, spidery, star-shaped flowers; some are fragrant! (left:* Brassidium = Brassia x Oncidium; *right:* Miltassia = Miltonia x Brassia).

TO REBLOOM, INTERMEDIATE- and WARM-GROWING
***ONCIDIUM* ALLIANCE ORCHIDS REQUIRE:**
Some direct sun.
Consistent water when growing leaves.
High humidity and good air movement.
Repotting before plants overgrow pots.

PAPHIOPEDILUM & PHRAGMIPEDIUM
The Tropical Lady Slippers

The Lady Slipper orchids are famous for their fantastic pouch-like lip!

KNOW YOUR PLANT!

Growth Habit: Sympodial, lacking pseudobulbs; thin, sometimes shiny, strap-like leaves (wider at base) from a few inches to over one foot long.

Flowering Habit: Spikes emerge from leaf axils on mature new growths. Some *Phragmipedium* rebloom at the end of the original flower spike.

Native Habitat: Semi-terrestrial, *not epiphytes*. *Paphiopedilum* orchids are native to the moist understory of forests in tropical and sub-tropical Asia. *Phragmipedium* are terrestrial, semi-terrestrial or sometimes lithophytic and native to forests from Central America to the north half of South America.

Light: Indirect light; no direct sun is required; most grow and rebloom easily as houseplants or with only artificial light.

Watering: Provide consistent moisture year round. Lady slippers are especially sensitive to salts accumulating in their pots.

Temperature: Intermediate to cool, depending on the type.

Potting Media: Semi-terrestrial orchid mix like used for *Cymbidium* orchids.

Generally Speaking

Paphiopedilum and *Phragmipedium* orchids are cool to intermediate temperature growing and native to the understory of sub-tropical and tropical forests.

As a result, they require less light than most orchids, preferring bright, indirect light. Even fluorescent lights are sufficient for reblooming. Also, being semi-terrestrial to terrestrial orchids, lady slippers do not like to substantially dry out between waterings. Lady slippers are one of the best beginner's orchids and make excellent year round houseplants.

SIMILARITIES BETWEEN "*PAPHS*" & "*PHRAGS*"
Both prefer bright indirect light; no direct sun or heat.
Both dislike impurities or salts in water.
Both prefer semi-terrestrial orchid potting media.
Both require consistent water when growing leaves.

Paphiopedilum

Phragmipedium

DIFFERENCES BETWEEN "*PAPHS*" & "*PHRAGS*"

Paphiopedilum	*Phragmipedium*
Asian (vast majority)	South American
Moist but well drained	Consistently moist environment
Cool to intermediate temperatures	Warm to intermediate (most)
Tolerate less indirect light	Prefer bright indirect light

Cyprepedium is another genus of lady slippers. Native to temperate regions of North America, they are one of the "hardy orchids" and are not discussed in this book. *Selenipedium* and *Mexipedium* lady slippers are also not discussed here because of their rarity in cultivation.

Check It Out!

The fantastic "slipper" or pouch-like lip on the flower is only one of the main attractions of the lady slipper orchids. Lady slippers are easy to grow and rebloom as houseplants, in terrariums, and under artificial lights. A single flower can remain in bloom for several months, especially when grown at the cool end of their temperature tolerance range. *Phragmipedium* orchids rebloom by producing flowers in succession off the end of their flower spike.

Lady slippers bloom in a wide range of colors from white to yellow to red to black-purple. Some lady slipper flowers are shiny, some have spots, and some have little hairs. Some *Paphiopedilum* have brilliantly colored leaves, and remain attractive as foliage plants when not in bloom. Long draping lateral sepals of some lady slippers (some to 3 feet long) create some of the most dramatic floral displays any orchid could offer.

Lateral sepals dangle from just a few inches to more than three feet!

For some international intrigue and orchid smuggling, look online, and check out the story of the "discovery" of *Paphiopedilum kovachii.*

REBLOOMING LADY SLIPPER ORCHIDS

Helpful Hints for Reblooming

Paphiopedilum orchids are often split into two highly generalized groups: *green-leaved* varieties that require slightly cooler temperatures, and the colorful *mottled-leaved* varieties that prefer intermediate temperatures and tolerate lower light levels. Hybrids tend to tolerate a wider range of temperatures, and all make great houseplants. Flowers last substantially longer when plants are grown as cool as they will tolerate.

Some Paphiopedilum *orchids have green leaves (left), while some have colorfully mottled leaves (right).*

Paphiopedilum orchids prefer less water when not growing leaves, usually during winter; that being said, the roots of *Paphiopedilum* orchids will stop growing in dry potting media (unlike *Phalaenopsis* roots, for instance). *Phragmipedium* like more consistent moisture throughout the entire year.

Once a month, water the potting media thoroughly with water only to flush out any excess salts that may have accumulated in the pot. Avoid water standing in the folds of the leaves. *Paphiopedilum* seem to tolerate frequent repotting and appreciate fresh potting media at least every two years.

When Finished Blooming

For *Paphiopedilum*, once all flowers have faded (watch for other developing buds), cut off the flower spike at the base.

Phragmipedium rebloom successively off the end of their flower spike when they are happy. Do not remove the flower spike until it starts to fade and wither; then cut the flower spike at the base.

Challenges to Reblooming

Do not let lady slippers dry out as much as other orchids. Lady slippers especially dislike dry air and thrive with good humidity.

Salts that have built up in the pot can harm roots and prevent reblooming. Water thoroughly without fertilizer at least once a month to flush out excess salts.

Avoid hot locations; provide a location with night temperatures at least 10-15F / 5-8C cooler than during the day.

Waiting to repot your lady slippers for several years can prevent them from reblooming.

new flower bud emerging!

Phragmipedium *lady slipper orchids continue to rebloom from the tip of the same flower spike!*

Lady Slippers are amazing!! Some have stripes; some are shiny; some have dots; some have tiny little hairs.

TO REBLOOM, ALL TROPICAL LADY SLIPPERS REQUIRE:
Indirect light; no hot sun.
Good humidity and consistent water.
Proper temperature and semi-terrestrial potting media.

PHALAENOPSIS
The Moth Orchid

By far the most popular orchid bought and sold is the Phalaenopsis *or "The Moth Orchid." They make excellent houseplants, bloom at any time of the year, and flowers last for many months. They even rebloom on previous flower spikes!*

KNOW YOUR PLANT!

Growth Habit: Monopodial; wide, thick, succulent, water-storing leaves.

Flowering Habit: New flower spikes emerge from leaf axils; reblooms from nodes on previous flower spikes.

Native Habitat: Mostly epiphytes in warm, lowland, tropical areas in southeast Asia to tropical Australia.

Light: Bright indirect light; avoid direct sun.

Temperature: Intermediate to warm; avoid temperatures under 55F / 13C.

Watering: Constantly wet potting media often results in the death of the plant. Avoid standing water in folds of leaves. Water more often when temperatures are high, less often when cool.

Potting Media: Medium-grade potting media; bark or mixtures of bark, moss, and perlite.

Generally Speaking

Phalaenopsis orchids are by far the most popular orchids to grow and rebloom as houseplants. The environment inside most homes already mimics the environmental conditions found in their native habitat: indirect light and average room temperatures. Everyone has a place inside their home for a *Phalaenopsis* orchid to thrive and rebloom!

Amazing!

Really amazing!

Check It Out!

If you've never grown an orchid, try a *Phalaenopsis*! The *Phalaenopsis,* or moth orchids, have miraculously showy flowers with intricately detailed markings. They are the most popular orchids as houseplants for several reasons.

They do not require direct sun; bright, indirect light is sufficient, and they easily rebloom under artificial light. Sounds like an easy-to-grow houseplant, right?! A red-colored leaf margin (edge) indicates the plant is receiving the maximum amount of light it can tolerate.

Each flower can last many months, and *Phalaenopsis* have the uncommon potential to rebloom several times from the notches or nodes on the original spike! Many people now prefer *Phalaenopsis* orchids over cut flowers, both in the home and in the workplace.

Phalaenopsis orchids can create keikis, or baby plants, from nodes on the flower spike. Once the keiki has 2-3 roots several centimeters long, it can be removed and potted on its own as a genetically identical plant to the original one!

Some members of the genus *Phalaenopsis* were formerly classified in the genus *Doritis*, and hybrids between the two were called *Doritaenopsis*. You will still see orchid ID tags with these names or their abbreviations (*D.* or *Dtps.*). Flowers are smaller while flower spikes are shorter and less curved. Some *Phalaenopsis* have been hybridized with members of the *Vanda* Alliance!

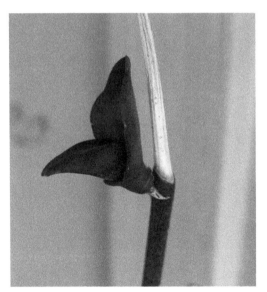

Phalaenopsis *"keiki," or baby plant, growing on an old flower spike.*

Phalaenopsis *flowers are not just white or pink!*

PHALAENOPSIS **ARE THE MOST POPULAR ORCHIDS BECAUSE:**
They rebloom with indirect light and average room temperatures.
They can bloom at any time of the year.
Each flower can last for several months.
They can rebloom on the same flower spike several times.

REBLOOMING *PHALAENOPSIS* ORCHIDS

Helpful Hints for Reblooming

Be careful not to break new spikes as they emerge along the nodes of the original flower spike. If you are not sure what or where a node is, see the photos on the next page and on pages 172-173 in Chapter 7.

Avoid constantly wet potting media, which can cause roots to rot. If you're not sure when to water, stick your finger down halfway in the potting media; if it feels wet in any way, do not water the plant.

Phalaenopsis roots will "run" a long distance in the search for adequate water. Lots of long roots on top of the potting media can be an indication that your orchid is not happy in its pot.

The difference between new roots and a new flower spike on a Phalaenopsis *orchid.*

Be sure to repot every few years. You'll often not need a larger pot, just fresh potting media. Because *Phalaenopsis* lack pseudobulbs, I like using a mix of medium bark and moss. The extra moss more easily hydrates the bark when watering, which is especially beneficial when heaters are on and humidity is low.

When Finished Blooming

Once all the flowers have fallen off your *Phalaenopsis* orchid, **begin by inspecting the end/tip of the flower spike**. If it looks green, fresh, and alive, I suggest you do nothing; it may continue to flower from the end of the flower spike. Again *if the end or tip of the flower spike looks alive, leave the spike alone, and do nothing.*

However, if the end/tip looks brown, dry, withered, and/or dead, cut off the flower spike right below where the lowest flower was on the spike. Nodes are found along the flower stem or spike, while the actual flowers are at the end of the spike. By only removing that part of the flower spike that had flowers, you preserve as many nodes as possible on the original flower spike. It is from these nodes that your orchid will rebloom.

*If you have already cut off the entire flower spike...*that's okay. If the orchid is happy it will make another spike in one of the leaf axils. You'll just have to wait a little longer. For more, see Chapter 7 What Do I Do Now That My Orchid Is Done Blooming?

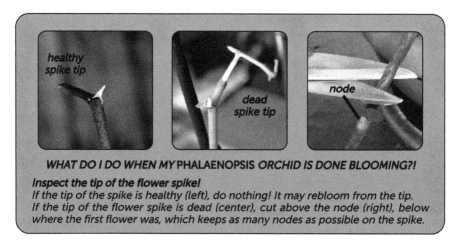

WHAT DO I DO WHEN MY *PHALAENOPSIS ORCHID IS DONE BLOOMING?!*

Inspect the tip of the flower spike!
If the tip of the spike is healthy (left), do nothing! It may rebloom from the tip.
If the tip of the flower spike is dead (center), cut above the node (right), below where the first flower was, which keeps as many nodes as possible on the spike.

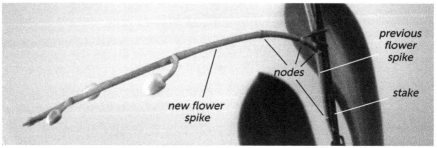

Phalaenopsis *reblooming from a node.*

Challenges to Reblooming

Watering too frequently or letting the pot sit in standing water is the most common reason *Phalaenopsis* orchids fail to rebloom and/or die. Remember it's not the excess of water that's the problem; it's the lack of air that causes roots to rot and the plant to suffer. Also, do not allow water to sit in the center of the plant or in the folds of the leaves.

Phalaenopsis especially dislike cold drafts and temperatures under 55F / 13C. There are few climates far from the equator that are warm enough for *Phalaenopsis* to truly thrive and rebloom outdoors all year long.

There is nothing wrong with roots growing on top of the pot; however, it can sometimes be an indication that the plant is not happy in the pot, e.g. needs repotting, has been overwatered.

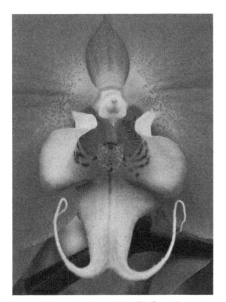 

Incredible detail on the "lip" and center of the flower.

Some Phalaenopsis *orchids can produce several flowers spikes with numerous flowers per spike = quite a show!*

TO REBLOOM, ALL *PHALAENOPSIS* ORCHIDS REQUIRE:
Indirect light and no hot sun.
Drying to some extent between waterings.
Warm or average room temperatures.
Medium-grade potting media.
After blooming, inspect the flower spike tip, and read p.139.

VANDA ALLIANCE
Vanda, Ascocentrum, Rhynchostylis and others

Vanda orchids have large, bold, vividly colorful flowers.

KNOW YOUR PLANT!

Growth Habit: Monopodial; leaves grow in a fan shape; some have the potential to become enormous plants with roots hanging several feet.

Flowering Habit: Bloom spikes (sometimes quite large) with long lasting flowers emerge from leaf axils.

Native Habitat: Epiphytes; widely ranging throughout tropical Asia and Australia.

Light: Lots of light with good air movement.

Temperature: Widely ranging, warm to cool, depending on the type.

Watering: Provide consistent water and high humidity.

Potting Media: Medium to coarse to very coarse grade potting media is essential to accommodate the roots' simultaneous and consistent need for both air and moisture.

Generally Speaking

The *Vanda* Alliance is a large group of potentially interbreeding genera including *Vanda*, *Ascocentrum*, *Rhynchostylis*, *Arachnis*, *Euanthe*, *Renanthera*, and others, even *Phalaenopsis*. Native to lower to mid elevations in southeast Asia; many tolerate very warm temperatures, and all prefer very humid conditions. Newer hybrids tend to be smaller plants than the *Vanda* species.

Vanda orchids may be grown outdoors in warm, tropical to sub-tropical climates. Otherwise they perform best in a greenhouse to provide proper light, temperature, and humidity. They tend to be difficult to grow as houseplants where light and high humidity are typically lacking.

Their long roots must dry out rapidly. Use medium to coarse to very coarse potting media, depending on the type. Small slatted baskets provide adequate air for their roots. Misting roots is beneficial.

 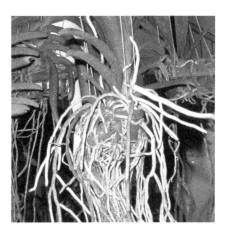

Slatted hanging baskets accommodate the potentially immense Vanda *root systems, sometimes without any potting media.*

Check It Out!

You will find an amazing array of colors and shapes in the flowers of *Vanda* orchids. Large, flat flowers display intricate details within the petals and sepals.

With adequate humidity, they are well adapted to life in a hanging or slatted basket that provides space for their large root masses to grow out and down.

Some *Vanda* orchids form keikis at the base of the plant.

Some orchids in the *Vanda* Alliance have recently been hybridized with *Phalaenopsis*.

REBLOOMING *VANDA* ORCHIDS

Helpful Hints for Reblooming

Be sure to provide lots of light, humidity, and good air movement. Many *Vanda* like it warm, but some like the blue *Vanda* (*V. coerulea*) prefer cooler night temperatures. Know your plant!

Provide consistent and regular water and regular fertilizer. Provide very coarse potting media when grown in pots so that roots quickly get the air they need in their moist environment.

When there are appropriate temperatures along with high humidity, grow *Vanda* orchids outdoors. They perform best in a greenhouse in temperate climates, because they really dislike dry air.

Vanda are typically not repotted as often as other orchids. Be gentle with the fragile roots when repotting. Very little potting media is actually required when proper environmental conditions (like high humidity) are provided. You may just need to add fresh potting media to what's been lost from the pot or basket.

When repotting, tall plants can be divided or "topped" by cutting off the top half and repotting it separately.

When Finished Blooming

Cut the spent flower spike as far back as you can without harming the plant.

The related Angraecum *orchids have huge, waxy night-scented flowers!*

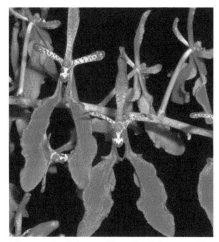

The colorful southeast Asian native Renanthera *is also related to* Vandas.

Challenges to Reblooming

Indoors, the combination of high light, high humidity and high temperatures can be quite challenging to create year round. Greenhouses work great! Grow them outdoors when environmental conditions allow for it.

Use the appropriate potting media, medium to very coarse. Remember their roots need easy access to humid, moving air.

Vanda orchids and their relatives typically suffer greatly from missed waterings, low humidity, and/or inconsistent care.

Vanda *Trevor Rathbone = look at that!! = truly amazing!! = I love this flower!!*

> **TO REBLOOM, ALL *VANDA* ALLIANCE ORCHIDS REQUIRE:**
> **Lots of light, high humidity, and excellent air movement.**
> **Proper temperature and consistent care; know your plant!**
> **Coarse potting media to provide humid air for their roots.**

ZYGOPETALUM & FRIENDS
Fragrant Fun!!

Many Zygopetalums *are extremely fragrant, similar to hyacinths and .... well, orchids!*

KNOW YOUR PLANT!

Growth Habit: Sympodial; very thin, strap-like leaves with egg-shaped, often shiny, pseudobulbs. Leaves typically fall off in less than two years.

Flowering Habit: Flower spikes emerge from leaf axils at the base of immature, funnel-shaped new growth, *before pseudobulbs form.*

Native Habitat: Semi-terrestrial and epiphytic orchids from moist forests at mid to high elevations in South America.

Light: Bright light or some direct sun, but not hot sun.

Temperature: Intermediate to cool temperatures; require similar light and temperatures as *Cymbidium* orchids.

Watering: Water more when growing leaves (even if in bloom); avoid water collecting in the funnel shaped new growth.

Potting Media: Semi-terrestrial to fine potting mix, depending on the type.

Generally Speaking

Zygopetalum orchids thrive and rebloom in the same basic conditions in which *Cymbidium* orchids rebloom. They interbreed with several genera like *Neogardneria* resulting in the common intergeneric hybrid x *Zygoneria*. *Zygopetalums* are an exception to the rule and bloom on new growth *before* the pseudobulb is formed.

Unlike most orchids, Zygopetalum *orchids create flower spikes on new growth before pseudobulbs form. Leaves continue to grow after flowers fade; water accordingly.*

Check it Out!

The South American "Zygos" have one big feature = fragrance!!! Not all Zygos have fragrant flowers, but the ones that do have an amazingly strong fragrance, reminiscent of hyacinths. Flowers bloom in curious combinations of dark purples, intense greens, rich brown (yes brown), and bright white.

Furthermore, *Zygopetalum* orchids have been hybridized outside their "group" with genera such as *Oncidium*, *Lycaste*, and *Epidendrum* among others.

REBLOOMING *ZYGOPETALUM* ORCHIDS

Helpful Hints for Reblooming

Zygopetalum orchids are an exception and bloom *before* new growth matures. Continue with regular watering after blooming; water less frequently after new growth and pseudobulbs mature, and until new growth begins.

It is not uncommon for the newest leaves to fall off pseudobulbs after only a year.

Repot as needed because they can quickly outgrow their pots.

Wow! Green and brown with purple and white!

When Finished Blooming

Cut back the flower spike as far as you can without harming the plant. If the flower spike emerged from *new growth*, continue to provide regular water and fertilizer as the new leaves develop. Reduce fertilizer and watering frequency after new pseudobulbs mature.

Challenges to Reblooming

Water collecting in the funnel-shaped new growth can cause emerging leaves and/or flower spikes to rot.

Inconsistent watering when growing leaves can prevent reblooming.

Heat damages plants. Avoid temperatures over 85-90F / 29-32C.

Do not allow water to collect in the funnel-shaped new growth, which may cause rot.

TO REBLOOM, ALL *ZYGOPETALUM* ORCHIDS REQUIRE:
Lots of light without extreme heat.
Consistent water as leaves develop.
Intermediate to cool temperatures.
Terrestrial or fine-grade potting media.

CHAPTER 5
THE ORCHID IDENTIFICATION TAG

THE ORCHID IDENTIFICATION TAG IS IMPORTANT?

Yes, that little plastic label is important for two reasons: it tells you what kind of orchid you have, and an orchid with an identification (ID) tag has more value to a collector than an orchid without an ID tag.

The Identification Tag and *The Name of the Orchid*

Knowing the name of your plant is the starting point for finding out how to take care of your plant. Without the name of the plant you will have no reference for how to provide proper light, temperature, water, etc.

Many orchids, especially hybrids, are difficult to definitively identify when they are not flowering. The ID tag of a hybrid orchid enables you to learn the background pedigree for the plant, which is now made easy with the help of the internet. If you know the name of your orchid, you can find out how to care for it.

At orchid show displays, the plant identification tag may be too hard to read; signs conveniently display plant names.

The ID Tag and *Value*

Some orchid enthusiasts consider the ID tag a big deal; for others the ID tag is not important. Both are just fine. I like to suggest saving the ID tag; it may come in handy someday.

Once you become an orchid collector, and I'm sure you will after reading this book, the ID tag represents a large part of the value of the plant. Without a positive identification and a definitive name, the orchid has considerably less monetary value.

The orchid ID tag is the most valuable part of your orchid. Don't lose it!

NAMING ORCHIDS

For your orchid to rebloom, you do not need to know all this "rules of naming orchids" stuff that I'm going to describe below. I simply offer it as a way to help you get to know your orchid better.

> **REGARDING ORCHID ID TAGS AND REBLOOMING:**
> **You only need to know the name on the ID tag...**
> **so that you know what kind of orchid you have...**
> **so that you know what care to provide.**

The naming of all organisms (e.g. spiders, algae, mushrooms, humans) follows a general rule called *binomial nomenclature.* In this system started by Carl Linnaeus in the mid 1700s, all organisms have two basic names: (1) genus [plural = genera], and (2) species, like *Phalaenopsis violacea* or *Psychopsis papilio.* His idea was to create a simple, formal system of naming that would reduce confusion. By simplifying naming, no two plants, animals or whatever, would ever have the same name. This naming system is still in place today and remains the worldwide standard for all taxonomical research.

Naming hybrid orchids, however, presents unique challenges. Many orchids have the capability of interbreeding not only *between different species*, but also *between different genera* (both in nature and through human-mediated pollination). The resulting hybrids display a huge and sometimes bewildering array of variability. Naming hybrids is therefore complex and technical. Luckily for us, orchids have their own naming system (distinct from other types of plants) to help us discern the different hybrids.

At this point there are a few terms you really need to know before understanding the rules of naming orchids. I am not going to use another source's definitions, but present these terms in my own way, the way I understand them.

Genus	a group of similar organisms sharing a common ancestral heritage. Capitalized and italicized, e.g. *Cattleya*.
Species (sp.)	a reproductively isolated group of organisms; obviously not an accurate definition when it comes to orchids. Lower case and italicized, e.g. *bicolor*.
Variety (var.)	name of one specific type of species. Lower case and italicized, e.g. *rosea*.
Hybrid	an organism whose parents are different species.
Grex	the name referring to a specific known hybrid or cross pollination. Capitalized and not italicized, e.g. Sharry Baby.
Cultivar (cv.)	a specific, single individual with unique characteristics; only reproduced by asexual propagation, like division or tissue culture. A cultivar may be of a species or a hybrid. Capitalized and in single quotes, e.g. 'Tolkien.'
Alliance	as it relates to orchids, a group of genera capable of interbreeding.

A *"genus"* is just one type of grouping of similar plants; a *"species"* refers to a more specific grouping of plants within in a genus, and is the most basic unit of taxonomy. For instance, all moth orchids belong to the genus *Phalaenopsis*. There are many different types or species of *Phalaenopsis*: *Phalaenopsis violacea, P. schilleriana, P. amabilis*, etc.

The definition of a species in its most basic sense is: a reproductively isolated group of organisms. That is, one species is distinct from another species, because for various reasons, they cannot interbreed. For most animals and plants this definition works well. It would be nice if this also applied to orchids, but it definitely does not.

Names Do Change

The International Code of Botanical Nomenclature (ICBN) regulates the naming and re-naming of all plants. As science "progresses" and taxonomic relationships are better understood, there arises the need to occasionally change names. More specifically, the International Code of Nomenclature of Cultivated Plants (ICNCP) regulates naming for cultivated plants like orchids.

For instance, in the early 2000s the four former *Cattleya* species and one naturally occurring *Cattleya* hybrid (*C. guatemalensis* = *C. aurantiaca* x *C. skinneri*) were officially separated into a new genus *Guarianthe*. As a result all hybrids with the new members of the genus *Guarianthe* had to be renamed.

When names change, it is common to list both the current and previous names. For instance, recently all members of the genus *Odontoglossum* were absorbed into the genus *Oncidium*. That is, all *Odontoglossum* orchids are now called *Oncidium*. This means that there are no more *Odontoglossum* orchids! Of course, names being what they are, I'm sure we will still see orchid species and their hybrids tagged with the name *Odontoglossum* for many, many years.

SPECIES vs HYBRIDS

Orchids can be considered to be of two types: (1) species: plants found (or potentially found) in nature, and (2) hybrids: plants that result from two (or more) different species interbreeding, whether in nature at by the hand of humans. There are different rules for naming each of the two. Here are examples to help you understand how to read an orchid tag.

SPECIES
Genus species, e.g. *Dendrobium unicum*

Genus species variety, e.g. *Laelia purpurata* var. *rosea*
A specific type of *Laelia purpurata* with pinkish flowers.

***Genus species* 'Cultivar,'** e.g. *Paphiopedilum delenatii* 'Jillian'
'Jillian' is a specific individual (cultivar) of *P. delenatii* with special characteristics distinct from other *P. delenatii* individuals.

***Genus species variety* 'Cultivar,'**
e.g. *Laelia purpurata* var. *werkhauseri* 'Kathleen'
'Kathleen' is a specific individual from the *werkhauseri* type or variety of *Laelia purpurata.*

INTRAGENERIC HYBRIDS:
HYBRIDS WITHIN THE SAME GENUS
Genus* x *species, e.g. *Cattleya* x *picturata* = *C. guttata* x *C. intermedia*
Hybrid of two different species within the same genus.

***Genus* Grex,** e.g. *Dendrobium* Emma White = *D.* Singapore White x *D.* Joan Kushima
Hybrid with a Grex name Emma White that refers to all hybrids between two other hybrids *Dendrobium* Singapore White and *D.* Joan Kushima.

***Genus* Grex 'Cultivar,'** e.g. *Zygoneria* Iron Knob 'Black Sabbath'
'Black Sabbath' is a specific individual from the Iron Knob hybrid that results from hybridizing *Zygopetalum* Artur Elle with *Zygoneria* Dynamo.

INTERGENERIC HYBRIDS:
HYBRIDS BETWEEN TWO OR MORE GENERA
Any hybrid resulting from a cross of two or more genera is designated in its own hybrid genus. The hybrid genus name is sometimes created by combining the names of the parent genera.

"Combo" Hybrid Genus

e.g. *Sophrocattleya* (*Sc.*) = *Sophronitis* x *Cattleya*

e.g. *Miltassia* (*Mtssa.*) = *Miltonia* x *Brassia*

e.g. *Sophrolaeliocattleya* (*Slc.*) = *Sophronitis* x *Laelia* x *Cattleya*

Another way to create a new genus name involves memorializing someone's name, with the suffix '*ara*' added.

Hybrid Genus, in memory of ...

e.g. Charlie + 'ara': *Charlieara* = *Rhynchostylis* x *Vanda* x *Vandopsis*

e.g. Potin + 'ara': *Potinara* = *Brassavola* x *Cattleya* x *Laelia* x *Sophronitis*

MORE ON TAGS AND HYBRIDS...

Some tags tell you only the parents of your orchid.

e.g. *Cattleya intermedia* 'Alba' x *Lc.* Ranger Six

Some tags actually do not tell you anything

e.g. *Oncidium* intergeneric hybrid

Ok, at least this tells you that the orchid is in the *Oncidium* Alliance. But the *Oncidium* Alliance is huge and highly variable. This tag does not help you determine, for instance, the optimal temperatures this orchid might require.

Some tags are even more cryptic. What does this mean???

e.g. G017.

Award designations are sometimes added at the end of the name:

e.g. *Masdevallia deformis* 'Perfecto,' AM/AOS

AM/AOS = (Award of Merit awarded by the American Orchid Society)

e.g. *Oncidium sylvestre* 'Mid Michigan,' HCC/AOS

HCC/AOS = Highly Commended Certificate awarded by the American Orchid Society)

e.g. *Phalaenopsis equestris* 'Candor Violette,' FCC/AOS

FCC/WOC = (First Class Certificate awarded at the World Orchid Conference)

SUMMARY

**Plants and animals tend to interbreed within their own species.
Science organizes taxonomy with "species" as the base unit.**

**A "species" is therefore a group of similar, interbreeding organisms,
that are reproductively isolated from other, similar organisms.**

**Orchids, however, are capable of interbreeding
not only between different species, but *between different genera*.**

Therefore, naming the resulting hybrids becomes a bit technical.

This all might seem a little complicated; by giving you a template of sorts, my hope is that you will be able to decipher your orchid ID tag. The more you know about your orchid, the better. Know your plant!

One wonders about the inspiration behind some of these orchids names.....

NAMING THE TOP 10 COMMON GROUPS OF ORCHID GENERA & HYBRID GENERA

Often on the ID tag, the genus name is abbreviated to one (e.g. *C.*, *D.*), two (*Sl.*, *Lc.*), three (e.g. *Pot.*, *Onc.*) or more letters (e.g. *Brsdm.*). Here is a simple reference guide listing some of the genera and their common abbreviations. Use it to help you determine what kind of orchid you have from the printing on the tag. Try not to be overwhelmed by the fact that this is just a teeny, tiny proportion of all the genera in the the Top 10 groups.

GENUS	*ABBR.*	*HYBRID PARENT GENERA*

Cattleya Alliance - some of the common genera

Brassovola	*B.*
Cattleya	*C.*
Encyclia	*Enc.*
Epidendrum	*Epi.*
Guarianthe	*Gur.*
Laelia	*L.*
Sophronitis	*S.*

Cattleya Alliance - a few common hybrid genera

Cattlianthe	*Ctt.*	*Cattleya* x *Guarianthe*
Epicattleya	*Epc.*	*Epidendrum* x *Cattleya*
Laeliocattleya	*Lc.*	*Laelia* x *Cattleya*
Potinara	*Pot.*	*Brassavola* x *Laelia* x *Cattleya* x *Sophronitis*
Sophrocattleya	*Sc.*	*Sophronitis* x *Cattleya*

Cymbidium	*C., Cym.*

Dendrobium	*D., Den.*

Masdevallia / Dracula

Masdevallia	*M., Mas., Masd.*
Dracula	*Dr., Drac.*

Oncidium Alliance, cool growers - some common genera

Cochlioda	*Coch.*
Miltoniopsis	*Mps., Mtps.*
Odontoglossum	*Odont.*

Odontoglossum are now considered as members of the genus *Oncidium*.

Oncidium Alliance, warm / intermediate growers - some common genera

Ada	*A. Ada*
Brassia	*B., Brass.*
Oncidium	*Onc.*

Oncidium Alliance – some of the common hybrid genera

Aliceara	*Alcra.*	*Brassia* x *Miltonia* x *Oncidium*
Brassada	*Brssda.*	*Brassia* x *Ada*
Brassidium	*Brsdm.*	*Brassia* x *Oncidium*
Miltassia	*Mtssa.*	*Miltonia* x *Brassia*
Miltonidium	*Mtdm.*	*Miltonia* x *Oncidium*
Oncostele	*Ons.*	*Oncidium* x *Rhynchostele*
Oncostelopsis	*Oip.*	*Oncidium* x *Rhynchostele* x *Miltoniopsis*

Lady Slippers

Paphiopedilum	*P., Paph.*
Phragmipedium	*P., Phrag.*

Phalaenopsis and related genera

Phalaenopsis	*P., Phal.*	
Doritis	*D., Dor.*	
Doritaenopsis	*Dtps.*	*Doritis* x *Phalaenopsis*

Doritis and *Doritaenopsis* are now both included within the one genus, *Phalaenopsis*; however, you may still find orchid ID tags showing the older naming with *Doritis,* mainly as hybrids with *Phalaenopsis*.

Vanda Alliance - some of the common genera

Aerides	*Aer.*
Ascocentrum	*Asctm.*
Euanthe	*Eua.*
Renanthera	*Ren.*

Rhynchostylis   *Rhy.*
Vanda   *V., Van.*
Vandopsis   *Vdps.*

Vanda Alliance - some of the hybrid genera
Ascocenda   *Ascda.*   *Ascocentrum* x *Vanda*
Christieara   *Chtra.*   *Aerides* x *Ascocentrum* x *Vanda*
Mokara   *Mkra.*   *Arachnis* x *Ascocentrum* x *Vanda*
Vandaenopsis   *Vdnps.*   *Vanda* x *Phalaenopsis*
Vandopsides   *Vdpsd.*   *Vandopsis* x *Aerides*
Vascostylis   *Vasco.*   *Vanda* x *Ascocentrum* x *Rhynchostylis*

Zygopetalum and related genera
Bollea   *Boll.*
Neogardneria   *Ngda.*
Promenaea   *Prom.*
Zygopetalum   *Z., Zygo.*

Zygopetalum - some hybrid genera
Bollopetalum   *Blptm.*   *Bollea* x *Zygopetalum*
Propetalum   *Pptm.*   *Promenaea* x *Zygopetalum*
Zygoneria   *Zga.*   *Zygoneria* x *Neogardneria*

COMMON QUESTIONS & ANSWERS
ABOUT YOUR ORCHID'S IDENTIFICATION TAG

Q: Why is the orchid ID tag important?

A: The orchid ID tag gives you the name of the plant. Once you know the name of your orchid, you have a starting point for learning how to properly care for your orchid, so that it will rebloom. The orchid ID tag also represents a majority of the resale value of the plant. Without positive identification, the orchid is worth little to a collector.

Q: What is a species?

A: In the strictest sense, a "species" is a reproductively isolated group of organisms. In a broad sense, a species is a group of organisms with very similar characteristics.

Q: What is a hybrid?

A: As it applies to orchids, a hybrid orchid is the offspring of parents of two different species, sometimes even different genera. Hybrids may occur naturally in nature or by the hand of humans (is there a difference?!)

Q: What is the difference between a species and a hybrid?

A: A member of a species is an organism whose parents are of the same species. A hybrid orchid results from parents of two different species. Some hybrids occur in nature; some are created by humans via manual pollination.

Q: How do I know if my orchid is a species or a hybrid?

A: Without the ID tag, you likely will not be able to positively identify the plant enough to know if it is a species or a hybrid - there are exceptions of course. Having the ID tag makes it a lot easier to answer this question. Generally speaking, a species orchid will almost always have two or more italicized words in its name, genus and species. A hybrid may have just one italicized word in the name of the plant…assuming the italicizing was done correctly.

Q: What should be on the orchid ID tag?

A: The full name of the orchid (see above) should be on the ID tag. The name of an orchid starts with the "Genus" name, sometimes abbreviated. The tag should also give a species name, a grex name, or a variety name.

The tag may also list the name of the grower. Unfortunately some orchid ID tags fail to give some or all of this information, which makes definitive identification difficult to impossible.

Q: What should I do with the ID tag?
A: You can leave the tag in the pot; be sure not to lose it. As plastic tags get older, especially if they have been exposed to lots of sun, they become more brittle. Once the tag breaks, you will need to make a new one. The printing can fade over time on the ID tag; use a pencil or a China Marker or wax pencil. If you begin collecting orchids, start a notebook. Record names so you have a permanent record of your plants. You can also record when they bloom, when you repot them, when divided, etc.

Q: But I don't like to see the tag in the pot, and I don't care about all this parent/hybrid stuff. What then do I do?
A: Toss the tag; no biggie!

Q: What is an orchid "alliance"?
A: An orchid alliance is a group of related genera capable of interbreeding, e.g. *Cattleya* Alliance, *Oncidium* Alliance.

Q: What if I still don't understand what's on the ID tag?
A: Take the plant and the ID tag to a reputable, independent garden center or florist shop and have them identify it. If you have a local orchid society, club or study group, attend a meeting and bring your plant and tag.

Q: Why does all this orchid naming stuff seem kinda confusing?
A: The naming of all organisms is based on interrelationships, starting with "species" as the base unit. The definition of "species" becomes vague and simply doesn't work when applied to orchids. Some orchids interbreed not only between different species within a genus, but also between different genera, sometimes many genera. With all this free hybridization going around, naming orchids is challenging. Lucky for us, orchids have their own naming system.

Q: Are orchids ever mislabeled?
A: Definitely. Even the pros do it. It happens.

CHAPTER 6
SELECTING AND CARING FOR A NEW ORCHID

You've made the decision to purchase a new orchid! Now you're faced with the exhilarating, yet sometimes overwhelming task, of selecting the right plant.

To start, the best method for selecting a new orchid (or any plant for that matter) is to have already in mind *the location where* your new baby will be grown. Then simply select an orchid whose environmental requirements for reblooming (e.g. light, temperature, etc.) match the location you have in mind.

What is perhaps less than ideal, let's say second best, occurs when you go to the orchid show or your favorite local nursery and become mesmerized by "that orchid I just absolutely have to have." You purchase it and then have to hope that you have a location with the right microclimate in which to grow and rebloom your new gem.

Once you've determined which kind of orchid you are going to buy, you'll want to be able to assess the overall health and vigor of the plants for sale. There are many features you could look at: leaves, pseudobulbs, flowers, buds, roots if visible. How do you select *the best one*?!

So many to choose from....how do I select the BEST ONE?!

HOW TO SELECT THE BEST ONE

Inspect the newest growth, leaves and pseudobulbs

Right away I look at *the newest/youngest growth* (leaves and/or pseudobulbs). How do the youngest leaves and pseudobulbs look in comparison to the previous ones? They should appear "perfect" and larger or potentially growing larger than the previous leaves and pseudobulbs. Are any of the pseudobulbs wrinkled? A few of the older pseudobulbs might be wrinkled, but the youngest pseudobulbs should look perfect!

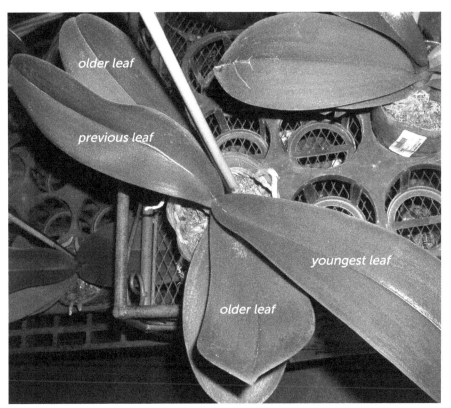

The youngest leaf (top one) is larger than the previous (older) leaves. This is one good indicator that this is a healthy and happy orchid!

Inspect the flower spike

Next, if the orchid is in bloom, look at the flower spike. *Are there any flowers and/or buds missing out of sequence on the flower spike?* The bottommost flowers on a flower spike (i.e. those closest to the plant) are the first to bloom, and the first to fall off; those buds/flowers closer to the tip of the spike should be the last to open and the last fall off. Flowers and/or buds missing in sequence on the spike means the plant has definitely been disturbed or traumatized in some way.

A flower is missing out of sequence on this Phalaenopsis orchid, and one of the flowers looks beat up. Avoid purchasing this orchid...unless you absolutely have to have it!

In addition, select a blooming orchid with *one or two flowers open and the rest of the buds closed*. With one or two flowers open, you know what the flowers look like, and closed buds means maximum blooming time. If all of the flowers are open and in full bloom, you don't know how long they've been open, and blooming may only last a short time. Unopened flower buds should look smooth and firm, not dry or wrinkled.

Also look for previous, cut off bloom spikes. If the plant is blooming right now, *and* has previously bloomed, it's likely a pretty healthy orchid.

Ideally, purchase an orchid with two or three flowers open (so you know what the flowers look like) with many closed buds (= lots of blooming time to go!).

Select the Largest Plant

For a given type of orchid, select the one with the largest leaves, growths, and pseudobulbs. Also select the one with the most leaves, growths, and pseudobulbs. The more pseudobulbs the better! Larger more mature plants have the potential to produce more flowers, and are more forgiving if conditions are less than ideal.

When selecting between two or more of the same type of orchid, and all other things being equal, pick the one with the most leaves and/or pseudobulbs. These two Cattleya *orchids are in the same size pot. The one on the right has more pseudobulbs; pick the one on the right!*

TO SELECT *THE BEST* ORCHID:

The newest, youngest leaves and pseudobulbs should look perfect.

Select an orchid with one or two flowers open and the rest of buds closed.

Avoid plants with spent flowers or flowers/buds missing out of sequence.

Select the plant with the largest and most leaves or pseudobulbs.

TRANSPORTING YOUR ORCHID HOME

Be aware of the weather outdoors when transporting your orchid home. Avoid extremes. During a summer heat wave or cold winter weather, get the plant home and out of the car as soon as possible. Locally grown orchids experience less environmental shock than orchids transported to box stores from distant tropical lands.

Many factors can cause "bud blast," or the falling off of unopened flower buds (see the section in Chapter 10 "Bud Blast"). From unfavorable environments, to jostling during shipping, to overwatering, any sudden shift in the orchid's environment can cause buds and flowers to prematurely fall off.

YOUR ORCHID IN ITS NEW HOME

The Right Location

"Know Your Plant!" In order to find the best location for your new acquisition, you must know what kind of orchid you have. Find the ID tag, cherish it, and keep it in the pot or in a safe location. Write on the tag the date you brought the orchid home. If there is no ID tag, make sure you identify the orchid. At least try to determine the genus, e.g. *Phalaenopsis*, *Dendrobium*, *Oncidium*, so that you have a starting point to determine what environmental conditions (e.g. light, temperatures, watering) your orchid requires (see the previous chapter The Orchid ID Tag and Chapter 4). Then provide a location with the environmental conditions that meets the reblooming needs of your orchid. In general, orchid flowers (and all flowers, even cut flowers) will last longer when the plant is grown at the cool end of its temperature tolerance range.

If your orchid requires full sun, do not put it outdoors in full sun immediately. Your orchid has likely been indoors at the nursery or grocery store for a week or two or more. Suddenly putting it in direct sun may sunburn the leaves. Instead, when you first bring an orchid home for outdoor growing, put the plant in the shade for a few days. Then give it a little morning sun for a few days; then a little more sun for a few more days, and so on until the plant is acclimated to the sun.

Of course, when your orchid is blooming, you can display it for a short period of time in less than ideal conditions (e.g. on coffee table in the middle of room); enjoy the flowers! When displaying orchids in the home, avoid locations near heating and air-conditioning vents. Use a humidity tray for supplemental humidity. Once all the flowers have faded, the orchid should be returned to ideal conditions.

Avoid displaying your orchids near outside doors during cold winter months. Cold drafts often decrease the life span of the flowers. Also, avoid keeping fruit near blooming orchids. Fruits give off a naturally occurring hormone that can make flowers fade very quickly!

Provide extra humidity

Orchids in commercial greenhouses receive ideal, computer controlled conditions in terms of light, temperature, humidity, etc. Once shipped, they experience a rapid shift from this ideal environment to a less than ideal environment (e.g. retailer, your home) with typically much lower humidity and light. Humidity trays (see the section on "Humidity" in Chapter 2) are one of the easiest ways to increase humidity in the air for your plants. Avoid misting indoor orchids.

What to Watch

In response to lower humidity and other factors, your new orchid in its original potting media may not like your conditions as much as it did back at the commercial greenhouse. Again, the *newest or youngest* leaves, growths, and pseudobulbs are your key to assessing the current state of health for your orchid(s).

Watch the pseudobulbs. If *only the oldest* pseudobulbs are shriveling or wrinkling, your orchid may be getting too dry or experiencing less than ideal humidity. That is, because the orchid is in a drier than ideal environment, the oldest pseudobulbs are shriveling and getting smaller, to provide water to the youngest parts of the plant. Another way of putting it, when water and/or humidity is lacking, orchids use the water stored in the oldest pseudobulbs to help the young part of the plant grow. As a result, the oldest pseudobulbs shrivel a bit.

If *all* pseudobulbs including the youngest ones look wrinkled, the plant may be suffering from underwatering, overwatering, or really dry air. If an orchid is allowed to dry out too much, all pseudobulbs will develop wrinkles as the plant uses the stored water. On the other hand, orchid roots die when overwatered. When the roots die, the plant cannot uptake water, and all pseudobulbs, especially the youngest ones, shrink and show wrinkles. If wet conditions persist, pseudobulbs may become soft and mushy (see also Chapter 10 Diagnosing and Solving Orchid Problems).

When blooming, do not repot

If your new orchid is blooming, do not repot it. Remember back in Chapter 2 we discussed that the stress and trauma of properly repotting your orchid, *while it is blooming*, can cause the flowers to fall off. If you absolutely can't stand the looks of the plastic pot in came in, set the plastic pot inside a more decorative pot and top dress with moss.

> **Avoid repotting an orchid when it's blooming.**

How Often to Water Your New Orchid

Unless the orchid seems really wet, it is generally a good idea to thoroughly water your new orchid once you get it home. As a rule I never like to tell somebody *how often* to water any plant. There are so many variables like light, amount of moving air, humidity, pot type, potting media, etc. By watering it thoroughly you will get a better base line on how quickly the new orchid in its new location is using water relative to your other orchids.

Remember that orchids in bloom will generally use much less water than orchids growing leaves. Seedling size orchids in small 2-3" pots will require generally higher humidity, more frequent waterings, good ventilation, and closer to ideal conditions than older orchids in larger pots.

ORCHIDS RECEIVED AS GIFTS

When we are blessed with orchids as gifts, here are a few tips for prolonged bloom time and continued overall health:

Look for an ID tag as discussed above so that you can identify the orchid and provide the appropriate environmental conditions for that type of orchid. Inspect the plant and assess the overall health in the same manner described above when purchasing an orchid. Are most of the buds closed? Are there buds missing out of sequence? How do the youngest leaves and pseudobulbs look relative to the older ones?

Remove any plastic sleeve, cellophane, or cache pot. The orchid can be left sitting inside a decorative pot without a drain hole, *if you are careful*. However, air has a much more difficult time reaching the roots, and the orchid may occasionally be sitting in some standing water, both of which are not good. Make sure the pot the orchid is planted in actually has drain holes.

There is no need to remove the orchid from this plastic pot, and there is no need to repot it while blooming. Once all the flowers have fallen off, go to the next chapter: What Do I Do Now That My Orchid Is Done Blooming?

COMMON QUESTIONS & ANSWERS ABOUT CARING FOR YOUR NEWLY ACQUIRED ORCHID

Q: How do I know what kind of orchid I have?
A: Look for the ID tag. You must identify which type of orchid you have, so that you know what kind of care it requires. If you can't find an ID tag, see Chapter 4, or ask a pro. Take the plant to an independent garden center, florist shop, or local orchid club or show to be identified.

Q: I want to buy a new orchid. What do I look for so I get a good one?
A: For a given type of orchid, buy the biggest plant. For monopodial orchids, look for the largest plant with the most leaves. For sympodial orchids, look for the one with the most and largest pseudobulbs.

If the orchid is blooming, select one with just a couple of flowers open and the rest of the buds closed for longest bloom time. If all the flowers buds have opened, you have no idea how long the orchid has already been blooming. Make sure the new growth looks absolutely perfect!

Q: Where is the best place to buy orchids?
A: Local sources are always best: local growers, independent garden centers, as well as local orchid societies and clubs, farmer's markets, and orchid shows. When attending a flower and garden show, buy from growers that are located closest to the venue. One can also reliably mail-order orchids from reputable growers in distant lands.

Use caution when buying orchids from box / chain stores. Orchids there may have been transported from great distances, and will likely be receiving less than ideal care during their time at the store.

Aren't you a plant rescuer?!

Q: I just got an orchid as a gift! What do I do?
A: First, know your plant; look for the ID tag. Figure out what kind of orchid it is, and provide the conditions the orchid requires for reblooming (see

Chapter 4). Remove any plastic, cellophane wrap, or cache pot. It is ok to display the orchid in less than ideal conditions (office desk, coffee table) to enjoy the flowers. Return the orchid to its growing location as soon as blooming has finished.

Q: I just received a blooming orchid as a gift. Should I take it out of the decorative sleeve? Should I repot it?
A: Yes, take it out of the decorative sleeve. No, do not repot it right now while it is blooming. Check if the orchid is sitting inside a decorative pot with no drain hole. Be sure the orchid never sits in standing water.

Q: I just got an orchid as a gift. How do I know if it's doing okay?
A: The *youngest* leaves, growths and pseudobulbs are your key to assessing the health of your plant. Ask yourself if the new leaves are emerging full and in good color?

If the youngest leaves look damaged, discolored, or disfigured in any way, something is not right with the plant. If young leaves, growths, and pseudobulbs are maturing at least as large or larger than previous ones, the plant is likely doing fine. Some of the oldest pseudobulbs may develop wrinkles if the air is dry or the orchid is drying out too much between waterings.

Q: I bought a *Phalaenopsis* orchid that I saw the other day - I just had to have it. The youngest leaf on top looks deformed and kind of curled, and there's a little hole in it. What's wrong?
A: It's always difficult to accurately determine the cause of a plant problem without someone diagnosing it, *in person*. But if you have determined that the youngest leaf on your orchid looks less than adequate, you have correctly ascertained that your orchid needs attention.

As a start: Did the leaf look that way when you purchased it? This is one of the main things we look for when buying an orchid - the youngest leaves. If the youngest leaves look damaged, discolored, or disfigured in any way, avoid that orchid, and select another one.

If not, how long has the leaf looked that way? Go to Chapter 10 Diagnosing and Solving Orchid Problems for further help assessing the health of your plant, or take your plant to an expert.

Q: I bought a new *Phalaenopsis* a few months ago, and the youngest

leaf on top is growing really big, much bigger than the previous leaf under it. Is that okay?

A: Yes; congratulations! This is a sign your orchid is truly happy.

Q: The new orchid I received has buds that look like they are drying up. OR The buds dry up, never open and fall off. What's going on?

A: "Bud blast," or buds falling off, can occur for many reasons. Sudden changes in the environment or over-watering are the most common causes of bud-blast; consult the section in Chapter 10 on "Bud Blast."

Q: I bought this orchid a while ago. All the flowers opened, and it was doing fine. Then one day all the flowers started falling off, and within a couple of days there were no flowers left. What happened?

A: Know your plant! Most orchids like *Phalaenopsis* and members of the *Oncidium* Alliance that produce a spike or spray of many flowers, which should not all fall off together at the same time.

Too much water, dry air, or dry potting media are some of the most common reason flowers prematurely fall off. Also keep fruit away from blooming orchids.

Q: I bought this orchid and the flowers only lasted one week. What happened? Why didn't the flowers last longer.

A: If the plant is happy, how long it remains in bloom, depends on how long the flowers have been open. Were all the flowers open when it was purchased? It's possible that it had been blooming at the nursery or flower shop for two months and no one had bought it until you came along. The flowers were only going to bloom for another week or so anyway. That's ok.

It's best to buy an orchid with most of the buds closed. If all the flowers are open, you don't know if they've been open two days or two months. If the flowers all opened at home, then suddenly fell off, read the previous question.

Q: My new orchid bloomed for a long time, and based on what I'm reading, it seems really healthy. What do I do after all the flowers have fallen off?

A: Continue to the next chapter, What Do I Do Now That My Orchid Is Done Blooming?

CHAPTER 7
WHAT DO I DO NOW THAT
MY ORCHID IS DONE BLOOMING?

This is probably one of the top five all time questions in the entire orchid universe. A lot of incorrect information gets passed around, and many orchid beginners are understandably confused. "What exactly do I do once all the flowers have fallen off my orchid?"

For Most Types of Orchids...

Once all the flowers have faded and fallen off, the spent flower spike (peduncle) should now be cut off; the next flower spike is produced on the next growth. Cut the flower spike as far down as you can without harming the plant. Leave a small stump so you can prove to your friends that your orchid actually did rebloom.

For almost all orchids, cut back the spent flower spike as far as you can without harming the plant. Leave a little stump so that you can prove to your friends that your orchid actually did rebloom.

With *Phalaenopsis* orchids, however...

Here's something fun: some orchids *will rebloom several times on the same flower spike!* Have you ever noticed the notches along the flower spike of your *Phalaenopsis* orchid? It is from these notches or "nodes" that entirely new flower spikes may originate. In fact, one reason *Phalaenopsis* orchids are so popular is because they have the potential to rebloom several times on the same flowers spike, when the plant is happy.

Once all the flowers have fallen off your *Phalaenopsis* orchid, **begin by inspecting the end or tip of the flower spike.** If it looks green, fresh, and alive, do nothing, because it may continue to bloom from the end of the flower spike. Again, *if the end or tip of the flower spike looks alive, leave the spike alone, and do nothing.*

WHAT DO I DO WHEN MY *PHALAENOPSIS* IS DONE BLOOMING?!
First, inspect the tip of the flower spike!

If the tip of the spike is healthy (left), do nothing! It may rebloom from the tip. If the tip of the flower spike is dead (center), cut above a node (right). Cut below where the first flower was, to preserve as many nodes on the flower spike as possible (see photo below).

However, if the end or tip of the spike looks brown, dry, withered, and/or dead, cut off the flower spike right below the where lowest flower was on the spike. By removing only that part of the flower spike that had flowers, you preserve as many nodes as possible on the original flower spike. It is from these nodes that your orchid has the potential to rebloom.

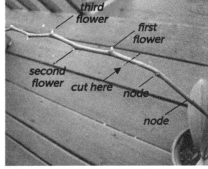

Where to cut a spent Phalaenopsis *flower spike? Cut below where the first flower was, above a node.*

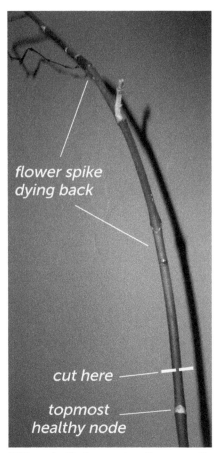

Phalaenopsis *flower spike beginning to rebloom from a node!*

Withered Phalaenopsis *flower spike dying back from the tip. Where to cut? Above the healthiest, topmost node.*

In less than ideal conditions the flower spike, may wither below where the first flower was. If the flower spike looks brown, dry and/or withered below the where the first flower was, cut right above the highest, healthy node. In general, cut off any dead, dry or brown parts of the flower spike.

If the entire flower spike on a *Phalaenopsis* orchid dries up and dies, cut back the entire spike they way you would with most orchids. See the first photo in this chapter.

You might say "But what if I already cut off the entire bloom spike?! What now?!" That's ok; it won't kill the plant. You'll just have to wait, probably a little longer, for your orchid to grow an entirely new flower spike from a leaf axil.

Other Orchids

Some *Epidedendrum,* some *Prosthechea* (formerly *Encyclia*), as well as *Tolumnea* (formerly called equitant *Oncidium*), and *Psychopsis* (in the *Oncidium* Alliance) are some of the other orchids that have the potential to rebloom several times on the same flower spike.

The cockleshell orchid (Prosthechea cochleata, *formerly* Encyclia) *reblooms off the tip of the same flower spike.*

Tolumnea (formerly equitant Oncidium*) reblooms from nodes on the same flower spike, like* Phalaenopsis *orchids.*

Both *Epidendrum* and *Prosthechea* orchids have the potential to rebloom off the end or top of the existing flower spike. Only cut off that part of the flowers spike that is *definitely* dead. *Epidendrum* orchids also have nodes on the flower spike, but the spike is usually covered by a dry papery sheath which can make it look dead. If you cut into the spike you may find that it is still fresh, alive, and green on the inside.

Then there is the amazing and magnificent butterfly orchid,

The reed-stem orchids, or Epidendrum, *rebloom from the tip of the same flower spike. Older specimens will remain in bloom all year long.*

174

Psychopsis papilio. This beauty has the rare quality of reblooming on the same flower spike *after a few years have passed.* With this orchid, the flower spikes are never removed unless dead and dry. *Psychopsis* will maintain viable flower spikes that can rebloom many years after the spike was created.

The Butterfly Orchid, Psychopsis papilio, *reblooms from the tip of previous flower spikes, many, many years later!*

COMMON QUESTIONS & ANSWERS ABOUT
WHAT TO DO WHEN YOUR ORCHID IS DONE BLOOMING:

Q: What if I didn't know, and cut off the entire flower spike on my *Phalaenopsis* orchid?

A: No problem; you certainly won't kill the plant by cutting off the entire flower spike. You'll just have to wait a little longer for it to grow a new flower spike from one of the leaf axils.

Q: What if the entire flower spike on my *Phalaenopsis* orchid looks brown and dry?

A: Remove any part of any flower spike that looks dead, dry, brown or otherwise not good. Start at the tip and work your way back. For almost all orchids the flower spike will wither, dry up and die soon after all the flowers have fallen off. *Phalaenopsis* orchids, however, have the potential to rebloom on the same flower spike. Therefore, it is not natural for a *Phalaenopsis* flower spike to quickly turn brown and dry and die right after all the flowers fall off. If this happens, ask if your orchid may be experiencing less than ideal conditions: too wet or too dry, low humidity, too cold, needs repotting, etc.

Q: What happens if I don't cut off the flower spike? OR What if I simply don't want to cut off the flower spike?

A: That's ok. You don't have to cut off the flower spike. There is no fairy god mother of spent flower spikes out there in nature that goes around clipping everyone after all their flowers fall off. For almost all orchids, the flower spike withers and dries up shortly after all the flowers have fallen off. For *Phalaenopsis* orchids, and orchids that rebloom on the same flowers spike, removing any dead and brown tips prevents further die back on the spike.

Q: What if I don't know what kind of orchid I have?

A: Look at the ID tag, and read the previous chapter. Try to identify your orchid from the information in Chapter 4. Take it to your local independent nursery or orchid society to have it identified. As usual, Know Your Plant!

Q: My *Phalaenopsis* orchid finished blooming, and it looks like it is growing a little plant on the flower spike. What is happening, and what do I do?

A: Some types of orchids (e.g. *Phalaenopsis, Dendrobium, Epidendrum*) can create a little baby plant (keiki) on the flower spike, much like your common spider plant will do. A keiki is simply a means for an orchid to propagate itself (see Chapter 3). The presence of a keiki *may* indicate that the orchid is unhappy in its current situation/pot, e.g. too wet in the pot (see Chapter 10).

Q: Can I cut the flower spike and use it in an arrangement?

A: Sure, depending on the type of orchid! Some orchids make better cut flowers (e.g. *Cymbidium, Dendrobium*), than others (e.g. *Miltoniopsis*).

PART 3

ENHANCING YOUR EXPERIENCE WITH ORCHIDS

CHAPTER 8

Know Your Microclimates:

Indoors and Outdoors

CHAPTER 9

The Origin of the Orchid Myth:

"Orchids Are Difficult To Grow"

CHAPTER 10

Diagnosing and Solving Orchid Problems

CHAPTER 8
KNOW YOUR MICROCLIMATES: INDOORS AND OUTDOORS

WHAT IS A MICROCLIMATE?

Whether indoors or outdoors, within any given space we find variations in the environment within that space. For instance, in a greenhouse, the area closest to the floor is cooler than the warmer space at the top. Inside your home, south-facing windows provide sunnier and warmer spaces than north-facing windows. These small scale environmental differences that occur within a given space are known as the "microclimate" of that space.

This outdoor patio garden has various elements with a combination of sun and shade, which create many microclimates suitable for reblooming many kinds of orchids.

> **"Microclimate" refers to the small scale environmental differences between nearby areas.**

What Causes Microclimates?

To understand the microclimates around your home it is helpful to understand the causes of these small scale variations in the environment. The interaction of light and temperature along with relative humidity creates a vast array of environmental situations. More sun means more heat. Breezes and air movements lower temperatures in a microclimate. The particular microclimate that allows one type of orchid to rebloom could cause another type of orchid to die.

Indoors, the orientation of your windows with respect to the sun, sources of heat, type of heat, and sources of water, all interact to create subtle variations in the environment. Sources of water like kitchen sinks, bathrooms, water features, and the presence of other plants increase the humidity of the microclimate in those areas. Sources of indoor heat and air-conditioning not only change the temperature but reduce the humidity in those areas.

Outdoors and in greenhouses, breezes, night/day, rain, etc. all create microclimates. Greenhouses let in a maximum amount of light within an enclosed, humid, but well-ventilated environment. This makes it easy to maximize light, humidity, and temperature.

GETTING TO KNOW YOUR MICROCLIMATES

Why Do I Need To Know About Microclimates?

In nature, different types of orchids live in different types of habitats (see Chapter 3). For each type of orchid, we must know how much light it requires, preferable temperatures, etc. Once we know what our orchid needs, we meet those needs by providing the proper pot and potting media and by placing the orchid in the correct location, or microclimate. When we provide an environment that recreates the conditions found in the native habitat of that orchid, it is guaranteed to rebloom!

To find the right location, you must become familiar with your microclimates, indoors or outdoors. Most of it is common sense. For instance, where is your sunniest location? Where is your coolest location?

A Maximum / Minimum Thermometer

As much as you should "know your plant," it is equally as important to "know your microclimate." A maximum / minimum thermometer records the highest and lowest temperatures over a meaningful interval of time (e.g. 24

hours) and can really help you to get to know your microclimates. Put one of these in a particular location; check it and reset it every morning. It will give you the low temperature that night and the high temperature from the day before. Many newer digital max/min thermometers have a second "remote" thermometer which is typically placed outside for simultaneously monitoring both indoor and outdoor daily temperature fluctuations.

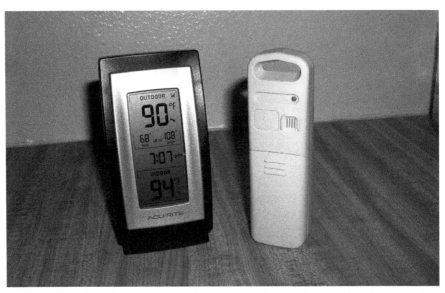

This maximum / minimum thermometer measures temperatures in two locations. The white box is a remote sensor that sends the temperature from another location back the main thermometer.

Using a max/min thermometer can be especially useful during the extreme (i.e. summer/winter) times of the year. In summer, a max/min thermometer will tell you, for instance, how hot that window in the bathroom gets where your *Miltoniopsis* sits. During winter, the max/min thermometer tells you if your attempt to be frugal with the cost of heat is why your *Phalaenopsis* has not rebloomed. Let's now look at how the interaction of light and temperature creates microclimates that help our orchids rebloom.

The Interaction of Light and Temperature - Indoors

More sun means more heat. A *low light and warm* environment is easy to create indoors; that is simply how homes are built. This is one of the main reasons why *Phalaenopsis* orchids are so popular; their native habitat is very similar to that found inside most homes.

One challenge is to find or create a *bright but cool* microclimate for orchids like *Miltoniopsis*. A few hours of morning sun hitting the still air in an east-facing bay window in summer, could literally cook an orchid. Moving air has a cooling effect, and a fan can be your greatest ally when temperatures are high.

Another challenging microclimate to reproduce indoors, *year round* is an environment with *high light, high temperature and high humidity*, suitable for a *Vanda* orchid, for example. As mentioned above, it is far easier to decrease any one of these three (light, humidity and temperature) than to increase them. Maximizing all three can be a challenge the farther one lives from the equator. By growing orchids in greenhouses or outdoors in regions closer to the tropics (i.e. similar to the native habitat) this microclimate becomes easier to recreate.

In temperate regions with hot summers and cold winters, one of the greatest challenges is finding or creating suitable indoor microclimates throughout the year. During summer, outdoors may be too hot for some orchids; the challenge then is providing enough light and humidity in your dry, air-conditioned indoor growing space. During winter, it's too cold to grow orchids outdoors; indoors, high light may be hard to provide, and the air is dry. On the other hand, the lower angle of the sun may result in more direct sun entering windows if large eaves on the home or deciduous trees block light during summer.

The difference in day length over the course of the year means you may need to move your indoor orchids twice a year. In fall, move orchids closer to the windows for brighter light during winter. In late spring move orchids away from windows that get hot during summer.

During winter, if your home lacks sufficient light for certain orchids to rebloom (like *Cattleya* or *Oncidium*), try to provide an environment at the cool end of their temperature tolerance range to nurse them through the winter months.

So let's take a walk through your house…

Your *north-facing windows* will be the coolest and will receive the least amount of light than any other unobstructed window in your home. Some windows that face north may not provide adequate light to grow *any* orchids, especially during winter. But very bright, north-facing windows may be perfect for *Phalaenopsis, Paphiopedilum, Masdevallia,* assuming that temperature and other environmental factors are adequate.

Unobstructed *south-facing windows* maximize the possibility for receiving the greatest amount of sun and warmth during the day. Save locations near south-facing windows for those orchids that require the most light like *Cattleya* and *Oncidium,* assuming again that the temperature is also suitable. In regions with cool, cloudy, short-day winters, low-light orchids like *Phalaenopsis* and *Paphiopedilum* may actually need the brightness of a south-facing window.

Unobstructed e*ast-facing or west-facing windows* essentially receive the same amount of sun. However, west-facing widows receive afternoon sun and are potentially hotter than east-facing windows. That being said, some east-facing windows, depending on their construction, can collect a lot of heat on a summer morning and "cook" an orchid within an hour.

The Interaction of Light and Temperature - Outdoors

In most climates, the temperature outdoors varies over a wider range than indoors. A maximum / minimum thermometer is an exceptionally useful tool for learning a lot about your outdoor microclimates. Take advantage of the automatic drop in temperature that occurs outdoors at night, which all orchids prefer. It can be challenging to recreate lower night temperatures inside some heated homes, especially during winter.

In the appropriate environment, in the absence of bugs and slugs, it is easier to rebloom orchids outdoors than indoors.

> **Grow your orchids outdoors,**
> **whenever environmental conditions allow.**

So let's take a walk around outdoors...

In *tropical and subtropical climates* many orchids can grow outdoors all year long. They may need to be moved twice a year to adjust for the year round variation in day length and temperature. In spring, you may need to move your orchids so that they do not receive too much sun and heat during summer. In fall you may need to move plants so that they receive more light. In addition, you may need to move your warm growing orchids closer to your home or under cover where it is not as cold as areas out in the open.

In the *temperate regions* of the world, it is simply too cold during winter to grow any of these tropical orchids outdoors year round. Some cold winter regions experience hot and humid summers that work really well for *Vanda* orchid...but only during summer. When it is too cold for them to be outside the other 4-6 months of the year, they can really suffer in a dry, low light, heated home.

In some climates, it may be too hot outdoors during summer to grow cool-growing orchids like *Miltoniopsis* and *Masdevallia*. Many cool growers like it bright, just not hot. You will find the hottest locations outdoors up against walls or other spaces that reflect heat as well as on hot surfaces like a cement patio.

You'll find cooler temperatures in breezy areas under the dappled light of trees or in locations sheltered from afternoon sun. Remember that moving air has a cooling effect. Reserve your breeziest microclimates for your orchids that require the coolest temperatures.

Humidity - Indoors

In their native habitat, the tropical orchids we're discussing experience humid, *moving* air. Most homes are typically drier with *still* air. That is, "dry and no breezes," which is the opposite of what orchids prefer. Indoors, this becomes one of the biggest challenges in recreating the native habitat of your orchids. The main cause of low humidity indoors are heaters and air-conditioners. Therefore, avoid placing orchids near heater and air conditioners vents.

> **If you must place your orchid near a heater vent, because it is near your only window or source of light, be sure to supplement the humidity near the plant!**

An easy way but horrible way to increase the humidity for our orchids is to enclose them in a plastic bag to trap the humidity inside. This might work for a very short time, because it does increase the humidity; but there is no fresh air. We want humid, moving, fresh air.

Create orchid-friendly, humid microclimates indoors by using humidity trays (see the section on "Humidity" in Chapter 2), and by grouping your plants. However, if too many plants are crowded together, air flow can be reduced to a point that plants suffer from stagnant air. Sources of water in the home create humid microclimates that we can use to our advantage. Assuming other environmental factors like light and temperature are correct, near kitchen sinks, in bathrooms, and near indoor water features are excellent, humid microclimates for reblooming orchids.

Humidity - Outdoors

The humidity outdoors is mainly determined by the climate in the region in which you live and the microclimate around your home. Orchids love it outdoors; the air moves and the temperature drops at night.

Of course, we can create more humid microclimates outdoors in much the same way we do indoors, e.g. humidity trays, grouping plants near other plants or water features. When orchids are displayed on wooden shelves or planks, watering or "damping down" the wood is an excellent way to supplement humidity for our orchids.

GROWING ORCHIDS OUTDOORS vs. INDOORS

OUTDOORS:

PROS	CONS
Wide range of microclimates	May be too hot during summer
Maximum light available	May be too cold during winter
Decrease in night temperature	More potential pests outdoors
More pest predators present	Storms and pets can damage plants
Fresh, moving air; easier to water	

INDOORS:

PROS	CONS
Easier to control temperature	Drier air, especially with heat and a/c on
Fewer potential pests	Less pest predators indoors
Less environmental disturbance	Less light available than outdoors
	Less fresh, moving air without a fan

Whenever possible, and environmental conditions allow, grow your orchids outdoors.

Cymbidium *orchids will not rebloom in hot temperatures. In addition, they require quite cool evening temperatures (45-60F / 7-15C) during fall and winter to rebloom. They therefore must be grown outdoors whenever frosts are absent.*

COMMON QUESTIONS & ANSWERS
RELATED TO ORCHIDS AND MICROCLIMATES

Q: What is a "microclimate"?
A: Microclimate refers to small scale variations in the environment of two nearby areas. Many different microclimates are found throughout your home, from home to home, as well as outdoors or in a greenhouse.

Humidity, and the interaction of light and temperature, create a number of unique microclimates. For any given microclimate, some orchids will be happy and rebloom, and other orchids will be unhappy and fail to rebloom.

Q: What is "direct sun"?
A: Direct sun means sunlight actually hitting the plant. Many types of orchids (e.g. *Cattleya, Vanda, Oncidium*) will never rebloom if they do not receive some direct sun during the day and over the year.

Q: What is a maximum / minimum thermometer, and how is it helpful for reblooming orchids?
A: A maximum / minimum thermometer (there are many kinds), not only displays the current temperature, but also records the maximum and minimum temperatures that have occurred since the last time you reset it. A maximum / minimum thermometer will help you understand and get to know your microclimates. For instance, it will record how cold it was the night before or how high the temperature was from the previous day, for example. Get into the habit of checking and resetting the thermometer at regular intervals.

Q: If orchids need to dry out to some degree between waterings, won't the rain harm my orchids?
A: Rain itself will not harm your orchids; they receive that in nature. Outdoors, moving air reduces the risk that water will sit in the folds of the leaves for too long. However, you will need to ensure that pots are not sitting in standing water.

If orchids like to dry out, won't the rain hurt them?!

In nature, and for orchids not grown in pots, excessive rain can't drown the roots of your orchids. Generally speaking, over-watering orchids indoors is more of a concern than rain on your properly potted orchids outdoors.

Q: Is it helpful to leave a window open?
A: That depends on what time of year it is, AND on your particular environment. Open windows provide fresh air and a drop in the night temperature which all orchids like. Open windows may not be an option during winter when temperatures are too low for some orchids. Otherwise, assuming that the temperature is appropriate, leaving a window open is an excellent idea.

As long as temperatures are appropriate, orchids love open windows for fresh air and cooler night time temperatures.

Q: Why does moving air benefit orchid plants?
A: As epiphytes (i.e. plants that live in trees), moving air is one of the key ingredients found in an orchid's native habitat. Growing in trees, orchids experience almost constantly moving air. It helps prevent orchids from overheating during hot weather and provides the roots the air they need, especially during tropical, rainy seasons.

Q: Where are the most humid places inside my home?
A: Sources of water create the most humid microclimates indoors. Kitchen sinks, bathrooms, washtubs, spas, and indoor water features create humid indoor microclimates.

Q: Where are the driest places inside my home?
A: The driest parts of any home will often be associated with heating and air-conditioning vents, fireplaces, and ovens.

CHAPTER 9
THE ORIGIN OF THE ORCHID MYTH:
"Orchids Are Difficult To Grow"

The truth is that many people still to this day fail at their attempts to keep an orchid alive for more than a year. Many people resign to this fact, and now that orchids cost about the same as a bouquet of flowers, they are purchased as "disposable home decorations" (see in the Appendix, "An Aspiration").

Everybody has been told at some point that "orchids are difficult to grow." Why? Many people hear that "orchids are difficult" and as a result believe "orchids are difficult." "If orchids are difficult, why should I spend any time learning about them, their unique habitat, or how they like to be treated?"

You've read this far through the book and have now discovered how easy it is for orchids to rebloom: simply provide the conditions found in your orchid's native habitat, and it's guaranteed to rebloom. Long ago, not much was known about orchids let alone their native habitat. Over the last couple hundred years, we've learned a LOT about orchids, how they grow, and what their native habitats are like.

Vanilla, the first orchid of commerce.
Source: Wikimedia Commons.
Author: Franz Eugen Kohler, 1897.

History of Modern Orchid Culture

The first tropical orchids were brought back to Europe in the 16th century as a result of trade and "exploration" of new lands. Toward the end of the 17th century, more orchid species were "discovered" as the continent of Asia was explored. Very little was known about orchids, and nothing was recorded about where

189

they were found growing.

By the 1700s and early 1800s, still little was known about these new, fascinating orchid plants being brought back to Europe. Orchids were grown pretty much by trial and error, and because nobody new anything about them, most died quickly. At the beginning of the 1800s, the belief that orchids grew in hot, steamy jungles furthered many unsuccessful attempts at cultivation. In fact it was this lack of knowledge about orchids' growth habits and native habitats that started "the orchid myth" that orchids are difficult to grow.

> **The lack of knowledge about the epiphytic character of orchids (that many orchids live in trees) started the myth that orchids are difficult to grow.**

Orchids seemed impossible to successfully grow; they were considered finicky, difficult, etc. The orchids that actually did bloom became worth small fortunes. As a result, only the wealthy could afford the expense required to successfully grow even a few healthy orchids. Throughout history, anywhere on the planet, whenever only wealthy people can do something, a mystique will develop about it. 'Orchids are difficult to grow.'

In 1809, with the founding of the Horticultural Society of London (later the Royal Horticultural Society), systematic research on orchids began that led to many discoveries assisting in the cultivation of orchids.

Fascination with orchids reached new highs once cultivated orchids began to thrive and rebloom, like the blooming of *Cattleya labiata* in 1818. By the middle of the 19th century, interest in orchids developed into a craze that reached manic proportions and spread to other European countries.

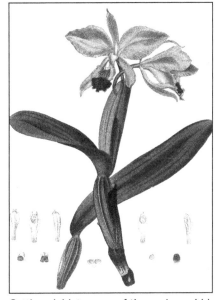

Cattleya labiata, one of the main orchids that started the "craze" in the 1800s!
Source: Wikimedia Commons. Author: Bernard M.

Collectors were sent out in search of new species, often ravaging, stripping, and burning vast areas of forest, making orchids even more rare. The collecting mania, hazards of transportation, and problems understanding cultivation caused the value of orchids to reach astronomical levels. Orchids became true symbols of affluence, because only those with wealth could afford these new, living, tropical novelties.

In 1830, John Lindley, considered as the "father of modern orchid cultivation," made the first definitive classification of orchids. In addition, he proposed that orchids should be grown in conditions similar to those found in their native environment! What?! Growers eventually realized that this fact was paramount to understanding how orchids to thrive and rebloom. Early discoveries included: realizing the epiphytic not parasitic quality of orchids, the use of appropriate potting media, better ventilation, greenhouses, observation of a "rest period" to mimic the dry season, and growing of orchids in three different temperature groups.

John Lindley: the "father" of modern orchid cultivation. He was also an artist!
Source: Wikimedia Commons.
Author: Author unknown.

Orchid prices remained high, because dividing plants was the only means of propagation at the time. Even though the first orchid seedlings were described at the beginning of the 1800s, little was understood of raising seedlings until later in the century. As pollination and orchid flower anatomy became more understood, hybrids were attempted and seedlings were grown. In 1856, John Dominy is credited with introducing the first artificially produced hybrid to flower, *Calanthe* Dominyi (*Calanthe furcata* x *C. masuca*).

In 1899, Noel Bernard discovered that orchid seedlings had a fungal symbiont that provided the necessary nutrition and sugars that the orchid seeds lacked. In the early 1920s Louis Knudson obtained the first seedlings

Calanthe *Dominyi, the first human-mediated hybrid to bloom in cultivation.*
Source: Wikimedia Commons.
Author: Walter Hood Fitch, 1858.

raised "asymbiotically," without a fungus present. In 1960, George Morel discovered the cultivation of meristem tissues as a method of vegetative propagation (a.k.a. "tissue culture"). This created a major production revolution that allowed orchids, and all plants, to be grown and marketed on the worldwide commercial scale that exists today.

Baby orchid seedlings growing in "community" pots.

Now we know volumes about the native habitats of orchids. All the hard work has been done for us. As a review, here are four key points described in Chapter 3 that were missing in the knowledge of orchid culture long ago.

Attribute of native habitat	How we care for orchids
Tropical	Provide supplemental humidity
Some prefer sun; some prefer shade	Provide light similar to what is found in the native habitat
Native to varying elevations	Provide temperatures similar to what is found in the native habitat
Epiphytes, living in trees	Roots require air! Let them dry out; not adapted to being constantly soggy

Why the Orchid Myth Still Exists Today

Science and serious orchid enthusiasts understand that many orchids live in trees (epiphytes) and must be cared for with this fact in mind. Those with this knowledge find orchid reblooming effortless. However, the fact remains that most people still lack this knowledge.

As a result, many care for their orchids like "regular" houseplants which require more frequent waterings and very different potting media. Lack of information results in over-watering and death which perpetuates the myth, that remains to this day, that orchids are difficult to grow.

Over the years and from various sources (see References in the Appendix), I've compiled a chronology of orchid cultivation for your reference and enjoyment:

A TIMELINE OF MODERN ORCHID CULTURE

1500s

1510   *Vanilla* is introduced into European trade.

1552   Orchids are mentioned in the Aztec herbal, *The Badiana Manuscript*, the first known reference to orchids in the Western Hemisphere.

1561   In Europe there are 13 known orchids.

1600s

1602   Orchids mentioned in Shakespeare's *Hamlet.*

1640   John Parkinson reports the presence of the North American native lady slipper, *Cyprepedium*, in Europe sixty years before the introduction of any tropical orchid species.

1698   *Brassavola nodosa* is the first tropical orchid cultivated in Europe.

At the end of the century, with the exploration of Asia, new orchids are brought back to Europe.

Brassavola nodosa
Source: Wikimedia Commons.
Author: Miss Watts and S. Watts, 1831.

1700s

1731   *Bletia verrucunda* is likely the second tropical orchid cultivated in Europe.

1753   Carl Linnaeus introduces "binomial nomenclature," the first coherent system of plant naming, and classification. Linnaeus' system creates a worldwide standard for naming organisms that was highly essential for documenting new species, cultivars, and hybrids, etc.

1778   J. Fothergill brings the first Asiatic orchids to The Royal Botanical Garden.

In the mid 1700s, Carl Linnaeus (Linne) created the system of naming organisms that is still used today!
Source: Wikimedia Commons.
Author: Alexander Roslin, 1775.

By the late 1700s some orchids were surviving and some had even flowered. Despite early successes, however, the vast majority of orchids perished, and Sir Joseph Hooker described England as "the grave of tropical orchids."

1800s

1802 R.A. Salisbury is the first to describe orchid seedlings.

1805 Dr. Robert Brown determines that orchids are epiphytes not parasites. However, the belief in the parasitic character of orchids persists for years.

1809 Royal Horticultural Society (RHS) founded in London.

1818 The first *Cattleya labiata* to bloom in England helps initiate the orchid craze.

1830 John Lindley completes the first definitive classification of orchids.

1852 The first edition of *The Orchid Grower's Manual* by Benjamin Williams is published.

1856 The first flowers opened of the first artificially produced hybrid *Calanthe* Dominyi (= *C. furcata* x *C. masuca*).

1860 The Wardian case is invented.

1862 Charles Darwin publishes *The Various Contrivances by Which Orchids Are Fertilized by Insects.*

1881 George Bentham publishes the first modern system of orchid classification.

1884 The first greenhouse structure is exported from Europe to Japan.

1885 First RHS orchid conference.

1899 Noel Bernard understands the role of a fungal symbiont in seed germination.

Conservatories and greenhouses greatly advanced the popularity of early European orchid cultivation.
Source: Wikimedia Commons.
Author: Henry T. Williams, 1872.

1900s

1906 The first issue of *Sander's List of Orchid Hybrids* is published.

1921 The American Orchid Society is founded.

1922 Lewis Knudson develops the asymbiotic method of orchid cultivation without a fungal symbiont.

1943   Carl Withner established the "green pod" technique of growing orchids from seed.

1954   The first World Orchid Conference is held.

1960   Professor George Morel discovers meristem tissue culturing.

1964   The meristem method of orchid cultivation is published.

1981   The red lady slipper, *Phragmipedium bessae,* is discovered in Peru.

1993   Dressler publishes *Phylogeny and Classification of the Orchid Family,* a definitive text on modern orchid classification.

1990's A new wave of orchid enthusiasm sweeps the United States that lasts for many years, resulting in tremendous numbers of inexpensive orchids flooding the market.

2000s

2001   Sparking a highly controversial episode of international intrigue, *Phragmipedium kovachii* is discovered in Peru. Check it out online!!

2014   Researchers find that *Phalaenopsis* flower quality and development improve with supplemental nitrogen all year, especially when creating flower spikes.

Currently orchids can be found in almost every grocery store, sold mainly as substitutes for cut flowers. The orchid growing industry has become so streamlined and efficient that millions of orchids are produced annually. To avid enthusiasts, orchids remain one of the most appreciated and revered of tropical treasures. Yet these days many orchids have the unbecoming status of "disposable home decoration."

COMMON QUESTIONS & ANSWERS ABOUT THE THE ORCHID MYTH: "ORCHIDS ARE DIFFICULT TO GROW"

Q: Why are orchids considered difficult to grow?

A: Orchids are commonly cared for like other houseplants. Most familiar houseplants like philodendron, peace lily, and spider plants require more frequent waterings and much different potting media than most epiphytic orchids. Lack of information results in overwatering and death which perpetuates the myth, that remains to this day: "orchids are difficult to grow."

Q: Can I grow orchids from seed?

A: Orchids produce the smallest seeds in the entire plant kingdom. The small size is a dispersal mechanism that allows seeds to drift like dust up high into the trees. The seeds are so small that they are easily susceptible to fungal infection. In nature young seedlings depend on a fungal symbiont to provide their nutrients. As a result, orchid seeds are extremely difficult to germinate and grow without special growing media and laboratory-like conditions.

Q: Can I grow orchids from cuttings?

A: 'Dividing' would probably be a better word than cuttings. Dividing is an easy way to propagate orchids in which the plant is literally split in half, much like common perennials like daylilies or bearded iris.

Sympodial orchids can be easily propagated by division, once the plant is large enough. Monopodial orchids typically cannot be divided. Orchids like *Dendrobium*, *Phalaenopsis*, and *Epidendrum* create baby plantlets, called *keikis*, that can be removed and planted separately as another means of propagation.

Q: Can I make my own hybrid varieties?

A: To create a hybrid, one will need to hand pollinate one flower. That is, you will need to remove the pollen from one flower and move it to the appropriate location on another flower. Then if a pollination event occurs, you will need to allow the seed pod to develop. That is the easy part.

Next you will need to find someone to grow the seeds in the seed pod. Look online for that one. Send them your seed pod, and they will send back your orchid seedlings grown on an agar medium in glass flasks. Over the years as you repot the seedlings, they will mature and begin to bloom. Name your favorites, and you've created new hybrid varieties!

I explained that involved task rather quickly. But think for a moment about the time and commitment you will invest. Creating new hybrids can be done by the home orchid enthusiast. It involves a lot of time (I.e. years) and work that will reward the one who proceeds *informed and properly equipped with the right environment, tools, and commitment required of the task.*

CHAPTER 10
DIAGNOSING AND SOLVING ORCHID PROBLEMS

CORRECTLY DIAGNOSING A PROBLEM
Is My Orchid Doing Ok?
When you first start growing orchids, you learn things like how much light to provide, how to water, and what temperatures to provide. Over time as you acquire a few more orchids, you'll need to learn how to repot them (luckily you have this book).

Then one day…you notice that one of your orchids doesn't look quite right. A leaf is yellow, the plant isn't growing leaves as big as it used to. You ponder, "Is my orchid doing ok?" The ability to recognize, properly diagnose, and correct a problem will greatly improve your success reblooming orchids.

I've answered literally thousands of "orchid problem" questions over the years and have distilled these questions into this Chapter and throughout this book. This chapter will help you diagnose plant problems and get you started figuring out "What's wrong with my orchid?"

I use language like "may be due to" or "could be," because no book, including this one, can for sure tell you what is wrong with your orchid. *Nobody* can 100%, for sure, tell you what is wrong with your orchid, *unless they are looking at it in person, or see a good photo of it.* You may ultimately need to take your plant to a specialist at an orchid club or garden center, and have someone actually look at your plant.

"Correlation Does Not Imply Causation"
Just because two events correlate or occur at the same, does not mean that one caused the other to happen. For instance, just because you see a bug on your orchid when your orchid is looking sick, doesn't mean the bug made your orchid sick; the plant might just be too cold, too hot, overwatered, etc. Correlation does not imply causation.

"Everything is Connected"

The problems you encounter are often not the result of one single cause. Multiple factors are often interrelated, and as it is said, "everything is connected." For example, lack of light will not only prevent reblooming for some orchids, but it can also increase the likelihood the pot stays too wet and the orchid additionally suffers from over-watering. Another example is using a pot that is too large, which prevents air from reaching the roots, which increases the chances the roots rot.

What You Must Know

To start, *the ability to differentiate between the oldest and the youngest leaves on any plant is a powerful tool to help you assess the health of that plant, especially with orchids.* For instance, it is common for the *oldest* leaf of an orchid, or any plant, to eventually turn yellow and fall off. However, if any of the *youngest* leaves look damaged or discolored, something is definitely wrong.

Being able to discern the youngest from the oldest leaves will empower you to answer questions like: Should I be concerned that this leaf is turning yellow? Is this plant getting too much water? Where will I see the next flower spike?

> **You must be able to distinguish between the oldest and youngest parts of your orchid plant to properly assess the health of your orchid plant.**

Next, *the ability to differentiate between healthy and dead roots greatly helps you assess the health of your orchid plant.* However, the roots aren't visible, unless the orchid growing in a clear plastic pot. So sometimes you will need to gently slip the orchid out of the pot and inspect the roots if you suspect a problem.

Healthy roots are firm, whitish-gray to greenish-white with a shiny green or reddish-green tip. Dead roots are soft, dry and/or and mushy ranging in color from brown to gray to black. It is common for *some* of the oldest roots to occasionally die. However, if all the roots are rotted, the plant definitely has a problem. An orchid is far more likely to recover from its traumatic event if it still has some living roots.

> **Assess the health of your orchid
> by taking it out of the pot and inspecting the roots.**

Symptoms / Possible Causes / Solutions

In this problem solver guide I present orchid questions / symptoms that indicate an orchid is experiencing a problem, followed by possible causes. I then give a remedy for the problem, and refer you to other parts of the book for more information.

There is an intentional repetition of questions / symptoms in this chapter from the **Common Questions & Answers** sections in other chapters. I have found that wording things a couple different ways often helps plant information "sink in" and become more easy to retain.

After reading this chapter, if you are still puzzled by your orchid's problem, take your orchid to a specialist at your local independent garden center, orchid club, or orchid show.

PROBLEMS WITH LEAVES

SYMPTOM: The leaves on my orchid look like they are wilting.
POSSIBLE CAUSES: The plant likely has a watering issue. If the plant has been underwatered, the roots may still be healthy, and the plant simply needs to be thoroughly watered. If the plant has been overwatered, some or all of the roots may have died. Lacking roots, the plant cannot take up water, and the leaves wilt.

"The leaves of my Phalaenopsis *orchid look like they are wilting. What's wrong?!" Inspect the roots!*

REMEDY: Ask yourself which leaves are wilting. Only the youngest leaves? Only the oldest leaves? All of the leaves? If only the oldest leaf is wilting, the plant may be lacking light, and/or has been under-watered, or nothing could be wrong at all. If the youngest or all of the leaves are wilting, it is possible that the plant has been over-watered (especially with *Phalaenopsis*).

Take the plant out of the pot and inspect the roots. If the roots look mostly healthy and the potting media looks still fresh but dry, put the plant back in the pot, give it a good watering, and provide ideal conditions. If the orchid is potted in bark, and the bark has become too dry, you may need to give it a good soaking for 20-30 minutes to fully rehydrate the bark.

If most of the roots look dead, repot the orchid, sometimes into a smaller pot. If all the roots are dead, repot into a pot that accommodates the size of the plant (see the section in Chapter 2 on "Repotting"). The appropriate time for repotting depends on the type of orchid you have and what time of year it is (see Chapters 3 & 4). Avoid repotting during winter. But if your orchid is at death's door, repot it.

When a plant is wilting, the inclination is to water the plant. Orchids, especially *Phalaenopsis*, can also wilt when roots have rotted from overwatering.

Wilting Plant? Which leaves are wilting?
Oldest leaves only = typically the plant will be ok.
Youngest leaves only = roots are not ok.

WILTING PLANT? INSPECT THE ROOTS!
Healthy roots on a wilting plant often indicate *underwatering*.
Dead roots on a wilting plant often indicate *overwatering*.

SYMPTOM: The bottom leaf on my *Phalaenopsis* orchid looks like it is wilting and/or turning yellow.

POSSIBLE CAUSES: If only the bottom (i.e. oldest) leaf is wilting and/or turning yellow, there may be nothing to be alarmed about. All healthy *Phalaenopsis* orchids will shed their oldest leaf once in a while. *Phalaenopsis* orchids maintain a greater number of leaves when conditions are closer to optimal (e.g. higher humidity). *Phalaenopsis* plants support fewer leaves when conditions are less than optimal (e.g. lower humidity; inconsistent water), but may still rebloom.

The oldest leaf (or two) on this orchid is wilting and/or has turned yellow. "What's wrong?!"

REMEDY: If the bottom leaf is still green but wilting and the rest of the plant looks ok, leave it alone. The leaf will likely eventually turn yellow and fall off. If the leaf is yellow and wilting, gently pull on the leaf and see if it pops off. Alternatively, if you really just can't stand looking at the leaf, go ahead and remove it with sterilized clippers. Cut the leaf as close to the center of the plant as you can without harming the plant. Be sure you are watering properly.

SYMPTOM: The leaves on my orchid look yellow/brown.
POSSIBLE CAUSES: Some large, specimen orchids (e.g. *Cymbidium*) lose a leaf regularly, simply because they have so many older leaves. Some orchids (e.g. certain *Dendrobium*) lose all of their leaves every year; some orchids have leaves that only remain a year or two (e.g. *Zygopetalum*). See Chapter 4 and Know your plant!

Is it the youngest or the oldest leaf that has turned yellow on these Cymbidium orchids? Left = oldest leaf is yellow; Right = newest leaves are yellowing.

Ask yourself which leaves are yellow. Only the youngest leaves? Only leaves on the oldest growth? All of the leaves?

If the youngest leaves or all of the leaves are yellow, it is likely the orchid has been overwatered (i.e. roots have lacked sufficient air). If only the oldest leaves are yellowing, the plant may be lacking light and/or has been under-watered. If only one or two of the oldest leaves are yellow on a large specimen *Cymbidium* orchid, there may be nothing wrong at all.

Leaves may also turn yellow (but remain firm) from too much heat, sun, or sunburn (see question below). Leaves may turn yellow (but mushy) from overwatering, frosts or temperatures that are otherwise too cold.

REMEDY: You may have nothing to do if only one or two of the oldest leaves are yellow. Use sterilized clippers to remove yellow leaves as they appear; plant enthusiasts tend to like looking at a green plant.

Gently take the plant out of the pot and inspect the roots. If the roots look fine, put the plant back in the pot and provide ideal conditions for that particular orchid - know your plant! If the roots look rotted, you will likely need to repot the orchid, sometimes into a smaller pot (see the section in Chapter 2 on "Repotting").

Always be sure you are providing ideal conditions for your orchids, and know your plant by reading Chapter 4!

POSSIBLE REASONS WHY
"THERE IS A YELLOW LEAF ON MY ORCHID!"

Oldest leaf is yellow	Youngest leaf is yellow
Lack of light	Too much water
Lack of water	Water in folds of leaves
Or nothing is wrong at all	Too cold

INSPECT THE ROOTS!

SYMPTOM: A few leaves fell off my orchid.

POSSIBLE CAUSES: What color were the leaves when they fell off? If the leaves were green, the plant may have suffered from over-watering, and/or had water sitting in the folds of the leaves that fell off. If the leaves turned yellow before they fell off, see the previous question.

Alternatively, some orchids lose all of their leaves every year, much like an apple tree. Know your plant! Larger specimen-size orchids have many growths at various ages and losing one or two of the oldest leaves once in awhile is no reason to be alarmed.

REMEDY: Take the orchid out of the pot and inspect the roots. If the roots are fine, be sure you are providing ideal conditions for that type of orchid; know your plant! If the roots look rotted, you likely need to repot the orchid, maybe into a smaller pot.

SYMPTOM: All the leaves have fallen off my *Phalaenopsis* orchid.

POSSIBLE CAUSES: A couple of times I have seen a leafless *Phalaenopsis* with healthy roots regenerate new foliage. But it's rare. Realistically, if there are no leaves on your *Phalaenopsis,* it's dead. At that point it's hard to say what happened.

REMEDY: Try again with a new plant.

SYMPTOM: One of my orchids has leaves that look "pleated," or has leaves with accordion-like folds perpendicular to the length of the leaves.

POSSIBLE CAUSES: Leaves with accordian-like folds almost always result from irregular or insufficient water and/or humidity. Lack of water and the subsequent lack of turgor pressure in the cells, prevent the developing leaves from properly emerging and unfolding. As a result, the leaves get stuck together. Sometimes a flower spike will even get stuck in "pleated leaves." This is a common problem with softer, thin-leaved orchids that require more consistent water and humidity, like *Miltoniopsis* and their hybrids. *The pleating or folds only happens when the leaves are young and not fully developed*; the folds remain for the life of that leaf.

Why does my orchid have leaves with these little pleated folds in them?

REMEDY: Do not pull on leaves to straighten them out; they can easily snap off. With proper water and humidity the plant will correct the problem on its own. The leaves will eventually emerge, but the "pleating" will remain throughout the life of those leaves. Be sure you are providing adequate water and high humidity as new growths emerge and the plant is growing leaves. *Miltoniopsis* and some *Oncidium* Alliance hybrids prefer a more consistently moist environment than other orchids like *Cattleya* and *Phalaenopsis.*

SYMPTOM: The youngest leaves on the new growth of my orchid are stuck together and are not unfolding and fanning out.

POSSIBLE CAUSES: When the leaves on the new growth are stuck together, it often indicates that the humidity is too low and/or the plant is not receiving sufficient water. New growths/leaves can also stick together when a plant has been "overpotted," (grown in a pot that's too big). The roots rot, the plant lacks a means to uptake water, and new leaves cannot "open up."

REMEDY: Know your plant! Provide appropriate water and humidity. Provide more water as new growth begins and when growing leaves; water less often when not growing leaves. Failure to increase watering

New leaves emerging but stuck together and not fanning out. Why?!

when new growth begins can cause leaves to remain stuck together.

Be sure your orchid is potted in the appropriate grade potting media and an appropriately sized pot. Check the potting media to make sure that it does not dry out too much between waterings, depending on your orchid. If the orchid is potted in bark only, soak the pot in standing water for 20-30 minutes to full rehydrate the dry bark (see Chapter 2).

SYMPTOM: There are dark spots on the leaves of my orchid.

POSSIBLE CAUSES & REMEDIES: There are potentially several causes of "dark spots" on the leaves of your orchid. Sometimes genetics dictate the presence of dark spots on leaves...they just have little dots. Some *Paphiopedilum* have naturally "mottled" leaves. Nothing is wrong; there is nothing to do.

However, some dark spots on leaves may be a concern. *Bacterial infections* often look like dark splotches that are sunken in the leaf tissue. Some bacterial infections display a yellow halo around the dark spot.

Oedema or edema appears like irregular shaped warts on thicker-leaved plants (e.g. *Phalaenopsis*) usually resulting from cold water, or watering in the evening when the potting media is already fully hydrated.

Viral infections on the other hand look like dark splotches or streaks that can be found on both sides of leaves and tend to be smooth or flush with

What are these spots on my orchids leaves?!
The top two photos show naturally occurring leaf markings; nothing is wrong.
(a) *Dark dots on an* Oncidium *leaf; nothing is wrong; the spots occur genetically;*
(b) *Natural mottling on* Paphiopedilum *leaf; nothing is wrong. Looks kinda cool!*
The leaves in the bottom two photos have a problem.
(c) *Bacterial leaf spot on a* Cattleya *leaf; spots are sunken into the leaf and may have been caused by cold temperatures.*
(d) *Possible virus on an* Oncidium *Alliance orchid.*

the leaves. Some viral infections like the Cymbidium Mosaic Virus can kill your plant. There are virus test kits available online.

I have found that when it comes to "dark spots" on leaves, it's really best to have someone look at the plant. Even from the highest quality photos in a book, "dark spots" can be difficult to accurately diagnose. The only way to truly diagnose the presence of a viral disease is have the plant tested.

SYMPTOM: There are these tiny little light-colored markings on the leaves of my orchid.
POSSIBLE CAUSES & REMEDIES: A few different bugs and pests can cause light colored makings on orchid leaves. **Spider mites** are teeny, tiny insects that congregate in little webs, often on the undersides of leaves. These insects (see below on pests) literally suck juices from the plant

Spider mite damage on leaves of a white sapote tree. Notice the tiny light green stippling on the leaves.

creating pale little dots or stippling on the leaves. Try releasing lady bugs or using an organic control for "sucking" insects like Neem Oil.

Unlike most pests who randomly discover your orchids, spider mites are often associated with dry plants, dry potting media, and/or dry air. Provide supplemental humidity (see the section on "Humidity" in Chapter 2), proper water, and a location away from heater vents. Hose off the plant to remove all webs, and clean each leaf with diluted lemon juice to remove all spider mites.

Thrips on the other hand create irregularly-shaped light marks by chewing in little patches on the surfaces of the leaves. Use an organic based product to control thrips.

Before using any controls, be sure to *read the entire instruction label and... DO WHAT THE INSTRUCTIONS SAY TO DO!*

Thrip damage on a Dendrobium *orchid; they eat the surface of the leaves.*

SYMPTOM: Are the leaves on my orchid sunburned?

POSSIBLE CAUSES: Some of the symptoms of *too much light without sunburn* could be: no flowers, lighter or paler colored leaves than the same plant in the appropriate light level; brown leaf tips, pseudobulbs shriveled. Some *Dendrobium* and *Phalaenopsis* develop a red edge around the leaf margin when they are receiving the maximum amount of light they can tolerate.

Sunburn however, typically occurs when a plant is placed in direct sun after having not experienced direct sun for an extended period of time (e.g. indoors during winter). Even plants that are native to hot and sunny, desert-like environments can get sunburned when placed in the direct sun, after spending time indoors out of direct sun. Sunburned leaves turn light green to tan to almost white. One sign of sunburn occurs when a portion of

The yellowish-white part of this leaf has been sunburned. Green parts of the same leaf indicate where another leaf was overlapping it.

an otherwise pale leaf remains green only where it was shaded by an overlapping leaf above it.

REMEDY: There is nothing you can do about sunburned leaves aside from changing to providing proper light. Feel free to cut off severely sunburned leaves. If there are only a few leaves on your orchid plant, I would suggest not cutting off anything, and just let the plant decide when to shed the sunburned leaves.

SYMPTOM: The leaves on my orchid are sticky.

POSSIBLE CAUSES: There could be a pest like scale, aphids or mealybugs on your plants. These types of plant pests poke a very tiny hole in the leaves, flowers, or buds; they suck juices from the plant and secrete a sticky sugary substance called honeydew. It's what happens when you get sticky stuff on your car after parking it under a maple or oak tree in summer, for instance.

Your orchid could also get sticky stuff on it from pest infested plants above them like outdoor trees or hanging indoor plants.

REMEDY: Look for the pest creating the sticky stuff. Keep the leaves clean and free of dust. Squirt a little juice from a lemon in a cup of water; dip a soft towel or paper towel, and wipe the leaves clean. By keeping the leaves clean, you can more easily see where pests are persisting.

Organic spray controls like Neem Oil-based products, for instance, control sucking insects on orchids like aphids, mealybugs, scale, and whiteflies. Before using any controls, be sure to *read the entire instruction label...and follow the instructions* (see the section below on "Pests").

SYMPTOM: Something is eating holes in the leaves of my orchid.

POSSIBLE CAUSES: Slugs, snails, or caterpillars are the usual culprits when you find holes in leaves. Grasshoppers can eat huge portions of your orchid leaves. However, because of the way their mouth parts are formed they eat only from the side of a leaf and do not create an actual "hole" in the center of leaf.

REMEDY: Iron phosphate is an effective, certified organic, slug and snail control; it's just a mineral, comes in many trade and brand names, and is safe around cats and dogs and nieces and nephews.

"Bt" is an organic, biological control that works only on caterpillars. "Bt" stands for the initials of the scientific name of a bacteria (*Bacillus thuringiensis*) that kills caterpillars by interfering with their digestion. There is nothing safe that controls grasshoppers.

For guaranteed success, and before you use any control, read the entire instruction label. Don't just "bomb" your plants. Get informed and be sure to use something that truly suits your needs.

SYMPTOM: My *Phalaenopsis* has little bumps in various places on the leaves.

POSSIBLE CAUSES: If the bumps easily fall off when touched, the bumps may be scale insects, either dead or alive (see the section below on "Pests").

However, if the bumps are hard and scabby and cannot be removed, you orchid may have oedema (or edema) which occurs when plants with thicker leaves (e.g. *Phalaenopsis* orchids, Ivy Geranium, *Hoya*) absorb more water than they can use and transpire. As a result, cells rupture from excess water leaving a permanent "scab" or blister. Oedema is often caused by watering late in the day or evening during cooler weather. Oedema occurs not only on upper and lower sides of leaves but could also be found on flowers and flower spikes.

REMEDY: The marks of oedema can't be removed and will remain for the lifespan of that leaf. You can't "do" anything to remedy oedema other than providing optimal water and temperature for that plant (see Chapter 4).

SYMPTOM: Each new leaf of my *Phalaenopsis* orchid is getting progressively smaller. OR The new leaves never grow as large as the leaves it had when I first got it. Is something wrong?

POSSIBLE CAUSES: It is extremely perceptive and important that you have noticed this. How the youngest leaves look in relation to the older leaves is a powerful tool to help you assess the health of your orchid plant, or any plant for that matter.

The new leaves on my Phalaenopsis *orchid are growing smaller than they used to be. Should I be concerned? Yes!*

When the newest leaves/growths mature at a smaller size than the previous leaves/growths, the plant must be lacking something, e.g. not enough light, too much water (= roots lack air), low humidity, incorrect temperatures, old potting media.

REMEDY: Know your particular orchid (see Chapter 4), and provide the proper conditions for that particular orchid. Use an orchid fertilizer, and be sure you are not under or overwatering. If you have not repotted your orchid in a few years, it is likely a good idea to do so at the appropriate time of year with the correct potting media (see the section in Chapter 2 on "Pots, Potting Media, Repotting").

PROBLEMS WITH PSEUDOBULBS

SYMPTOM: The leaves are falling off the pseudobulbs on my orchid.

POSSIBLE CAUSES: Which pseudobulbs, the youngest or the oldest ones? Are all of the leaves falling off? The oldest pseudobulbs will lose their leaves at some point and, it may not be a concern. I would definitely be alarmed if leaves are falling off one of the youngest pseudobulbs.

Remember to know your plant! Some orchids' leaves fall off each year (e.g. some *Dendrobium*); some orchids' leaves fall off after a year or two (e.g. *Zygopetalum*); and some orchids' leaves last for several years (e.g. *Cattleya, Cymbidium*).

REMEDY: If the leaves are falling off the oldest pseudobulbs only, be sure the orchid is receiving proper water and light; otherwise do nothing.

If the leaves are falling off younger pseudobulbs, something is likely wrong with the roots. Take the plant out of the pot and inspect the roots. If the roots look fine, be sure you are giving the orchid ideal care (see Chapter 4); if the roots look rotted, the orchid may have been overwatered or lacked sufficient light and now requires repotting to save it (see the section in Chapter 2 on "Pots, Potting Media and Repotting").

SYMPTOM: The pseudobulbs on my orchid look wrinkled.

POSSIBLE CAUSES: Pseudobulbs are water storing organs for the plant that help the plant survive when water is lacking (see Chapter 3). The pseudobulbs will only shrivel or develop wrinkles when the plant is

Why are all the pseudobulbs on my orchid wrinkled?

experiencing conditions outside its comfort zone, e.g. too dry, too wet, too hot, too cold, etc.

If water/humidity is lacking, the *oldest* pseudobulbs will shrivel first to provide water to the younger, actively growing parts of the plant. If only the *youngest* pseudobulbs are wrinkled and shriveled, water may have sat in the folds of the leaves on that new growth, or the plant may have been over-watered. If *all* pseudobulbs have shriveled, the same thing may have happened or the plant may be lacking humidity and water. All pseudobulbs shriveling commonly happens to newly purchased orchids that go from the ideal conditions at the growers to the grocery store to a dry heated/air-conditioned home.

Then again, some orchids have pseudobulbs that naturally look wrinkled. Know your plant!

REMEDY: Inspect the roots! If most of the roots are firm and healthy, the pseudobulbs may have shriveled from lack of water or dry air. Be sure you're providing adequate water and optimal humidity.

If most roots are dead, soft, and mushy, or if there are only one or a few living roots, the orchid has likely have been overwatered and/or needs repotting (see Chapter 2).

SYMPTOM: The pseudobulbs on my orchid look all soft and mushy.

POSSIBLE CAUSES: Pseudobulbs typically become *soft and mushy* for two reasons: (1) overwatering (i.e. roots lacking air) or water sitting in the folds of the leaves, or (2) the plant has experienced frosts or temperatures that are too cold.

REMEDY: Inspect the roots. If the roots appear healthy, put the plant back in the pot, provide ideal conditions, and remove dead pseudobulbs with sterilized clippers (see Chapter 4). If most or all of the roots appear soft, mushy, and dead you will probably need to be repot the orchid, perhaps into a smaller pot (see Chapter 2). If all the roots and pseudobulbs are dead, the plant is dead. Yep.

SYMPTOM: It looks like just a couple of the oldest pseudobulbs are shriveled on my orchid,

POSSIBLE CAUSES: For even healthy orchids, it is not uncommon for the oldest pseudobulb to shrivel and die once in a while. The oldest pseudobulbs are least valuable to the plant. During environmental stresses, the plant may utilize the water stores in these oldest pseudobulbs. If the oldest pseudobulbs have been dead a long time, you will likely not be able to determine what happened. Diagnose problems right away.

REMEDY: Inspect the roots. It is likely that the oldest roots associated with the shriveled pseudobulbs are dead. If the roots appear healthy, put the plant back in the pot and provide ideal conditions (see Chapter 4). If most of the roots on the whole plant seem dead, repot the orchid at the appropriate time (see Chapter 2).

SYMPTOM: Some of the older pseudobulbs appear dry and hollow

POSSIBLE CAUSES: It is not uncommon for the oldest pseudobulbs to eventually shrivel and dry up, typically years down the road. If just one or two of the oldest pseudobulbs are dry and hollow, you may have nothing to do at all. The old, dead pseudobulbs can be carefully removed now, or be removed during the next repotting.

REMEDY: As usual, gently take the orchid out of the pot and inspect the roots. Are there any living roots? If the roots are firm and healthy, the plant may have been lacking water or humidity. If the plant has numerous pseudobulbs and only one or two of the older ones are dry and hollow, nothing may be wrong at all.

Be sure you're providing optimal humidity. If most of the roots appear soft and mushy, or if there are only one or a few living roots, the orchid may have been overwatered and/or may need repotting (see Chapter 2).

SYMPTOM: There appears to be a new growth/shoot growing off the top/side of the pseudobulb.

POSSIBLE CAUSES: Many orchids are capable of creating new growths on the top or sides of pseudobulbs (e.g. *Dendrobium, Epidendrum*), and even on

flower spikes (e.g. *Phalaenopsis*). This growth is called a "keiki" (see Chapter 3), and allows the plant to propagate itself. Sometimes, but certainly not always, an orchid creates a keiki, because it is unhappy in the pot (e.g. old potting media, overwatering); it is trying to create the possibility to grow somewhere else (i.e. not in the pot).

Dendrobium *growing "keikis" or baby plants off stem-shaped pseudobulbs.*

REMEDY: There is nothing to do. If you simply don't like the look of the keiki, you can remove it. Once the keiki has a few roots that are a few inches long, the keiki can be removed with a sterilized clippers or knife, and be repotted. The keiki will be an exact genetic replica of the original plant.

At the same time be sure that you are providing ideal conditions. If the plant looks healthy and several years have passed since you last repotted it, do so at the next appropriate time.

SYMPTOM: The newest pseudobulbs are smaller than previous pseudobulbs.

POSSIBLE CAUSES: If your orchid is happy, each new growth and pseudobulb should grow to be at least as large, but hopefully larger, than the previously grown pseudobulb(s). If the newest pseudobulbs are maturing smaller than the previous ones, the plant must be lacking something, e.g. not enough light, water, air, proper potting media, etc. You are extremely observant to have noticed this.

REMEDY: Know your plant! Provide the proper conditions for that orchid, especially light. Be sure you are not under or overwatering. If you have not repotted your orchid in the last couple of years, do so at the appropriate time. (see Chapters 2 & 4).

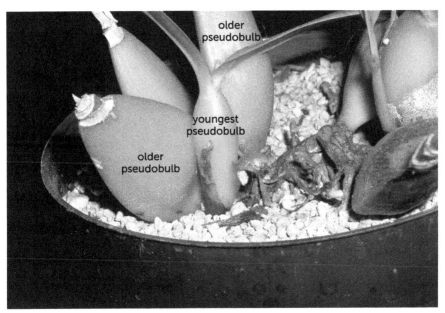

The youngest pseudobulb on this orchid has matured much smaller than the older, previous pseudobulbs. Something is not quite right...

PROBLEMS WITH FLOWERS AND FLOWER BUDS

SYMPTOM: The flower buds on my orchid fell off before they opened.

POSSIBLE CAUSES: When flower buds fall off before they open, it's called "bud blast".

REMEDY: Refer to the bud blast chart below, and correct the situation.

This flower bud looks wrinkled and is not going to open = "bud blast".

CAUSES OF BUD BLAST
When flowers buds fall off before they open

Extreme air or water temperatures outside the suitable range, e.g. cold drafts.

Sudden temperatures fluctuations (e.g. bringing a budded *Cymbidium* orchid into a heated house in the fall to protect it from frost).

Watering too frequently when your orchid is growing a flower spike, especially with *Cymbidium* and *Dendrobium.* Many orchids require less water when in bud or bloom, and when not growing leaves.

Humidity too low. Proximity to heater vents and air conditioners.

Physical disturbance to flower buds - shipping, being bumped.

Polluted air from car exhaust or heaters, for example.

Presence of ethylene, a naturally occurring plant hormone in fruit. Keep blooming orchids away from bowls of fruit as well as fruit scraps, especially bananas, apples, avocados, peaches, pears.

SYMPTOM: Some of the flower buds look like they are wilting or dried up; they never opened and fell off.
POSSIBLE CAUSES: See possible causes of bud blast in the chart above.
REMEDY: Refer to the bud blast chart above, and correct the situation.

SYMPTOM: All of the flowers suddenly fell off my orchid.
POSSIBLE CAUSES: Flowers can fall off for the same reasons that unopened flower buds fall off.
REMEDY: Refer to the bud blast chart above, and correct the situation.

SYMPTOM: A couple of flowers have fallen off my orchid.
POSSIBLE CAUSES: There may be nothing wrong at all if only a couple of flowers have fallen off your orchid. The questions to ask is which flowers have fallen off?

Typically, the flowers that open first (those on the spike closest to the plant) are the same flowers that fall off first. The flowers should ideally fall off in sequence starting with the flower lowest on the spike that opened first (closest to the plant), proceeding toward the tip to the flowers that opened last (farthest from the plant). As with leaves, we may not need to be concerned when the oldest flower falls off.

Some of the older flowers have fallen off for these two orchids.

However, when the youngest flower(s) near the tip of the spike fall off before the other flowers, out of sequence, you have a reason to be concerned. Flowers fall off out of sequence for the same reasons as bud blast.

A few flower buds are missing from this Phalaenopsis *flower spike before the oldest buds have opened. Something happened...I wouldn't buy it.*

REMEDY: If the flowers that have fallen off the are first ones that opened, then there is likely nothing to do; the flowers may be simply spent. Be sure you are providing ideal care for your plant (see Chapters 2 and 6).

If a few flowers have fallen off out of sequence, be sure you are providing ideal conditions: proper humidity, not too wet, no cold drafts, etc., and refer to the bud blast chart above.

SYMPTOM: The flowers on my orchid opened and has these spots and/ or streaks.

POSSIBLE CAUSES: There are several possible causes for what you are describing. Because of the subtleties involved in describing "spots" or "streaks," it may be difficult to positively determine the cause. Here are a few possibilities:

Thrips can live inside flower buds and eat the soft tissue of the unopened flower. When the buds open, the flower petals and sepals are streaked with irregular light patches.

Viral infections like the Odontoglossum ringspot virus (ORSV - yellow splotches with dark spots) or Blossom Necrotic Streak (irregular patches with flower color absent) can also produce similarly marked flowers.

REMEDY: It is probably best to have an expert look at your orchid. The only way to know for sure if your orchid has a viral infection is to get the plant tested. Online you can purchase strip test kits for the two main viruses Cymbidium Mosaic Virus (CMV) and ORSV.

Failure to sterilize clippers is by far the most common way viruses and viral infections are transmitted from plant to plant. Be sure to sterilize all clippers with flame (best) or alcohol each time you start cutting on a different plant.

SYMPTOM: The flowers on my orchid look splotchy. OR The color on my orchid flowers (often *Cattleya* relatives) looks patchy or like there are streaks of color rather than solid color.

POSSIBLE CAUSES: The flowers could have what is called "color break" also caused by a viral infection. Here flowers are sometimes malformed, sometimes not, and have light and/or dark colored patches.

REMEDY: See remedy to previous question.

SYMPTOM: It looks like something is eating (or has eaten) the flowers on my orchid.

POSSIBLE CAUSES: Slugs, snails, or caterpillars are frequent culprits when it come to holes in flowers. Other possible pests include grasshoppers and earwigs. See also the next section on "Pests."

REMEDY: Slug and snail controls are available, some for organic gardening. *Iron phosphate* (a mineral) is a common organic control (with many brand names) that kills slugs and snails but is safe around pets and wildlife.

"Bt" is an organic, biological control that works only on caterpillars. "Bt" stands for the initials of the scientific name of a bacteria (*Bacillus thuringiensis*) that kills caterpillars by interfering with their digestion.

Before you use any control, be sure to read the entire instruction label, and be sure to use something that truly suits your needs. You may need to have someone look at your orchid to determine who is eating your flowers.

PROBLEMS WITH PESTS

GOT BUGS?!

Most bugs and pests occur randomly on a plant. Usually, but not always, you have not done anything to attract the bugs to your plant; they have simply showed up.

For this reason, and others, when it comes to your orchids not reblooming, I believe that pests are far less of an issue than the five main reasons discussed in Chapter 2. In the September 2015 issue of *Orchids* magazine, Sue Bottom corroborates my observations: "I have come to believe that there are more physiological and cultural issues that cause problems with your orchids than those caused by pests and disease."

Nonetheless, bugs do occur, and orchid enthusiasts need to know what to do about them.

Using Pest Controls

First, be sure you know what kind of bug, pest, or disease you are dealing with. Then, be sure you use a control that says on the label that it will control that particular bug, pest, or disease.

Controls differ for *"sucking" insects* (e.g. aphids, scale, mealybugs), versus *"chewing" insects* (e.g. caterpillars, thrips, beetles), versus *slugs / snails*. Consider also that controls (whether organic or otherwise) kill bugs; they do not fix holes or repair missing parts of leaves.

USE DIFFERENT CONTROLS FOR:
(1) *sucking insects* that literally suck sugary juices out of the plant.
e.g. aphids, mealybugs, whitefly, scale
(2) *chewing insects* that actually eat and remove parts of the plant.
e.g. caterpillars, thrips, beetles, leaf miners
(3) slugs and snails

Keep your plant clean by removing dead/living bugs, so you can see where any living ones may still be hiding. Cotton swabs or soft paper towels work great for removing bugs; avoid abrasive cleanings with a toothbrush, for instance.

> **BEFORE USING ANY CONTROLS, READ THE ENTIRE LABEL.**
> **Understand...**
> **(1) when and when not to apply,**
> **(2) how to apply, and**
> **(3) how often to reapply.**
> **FOLLOW THE INSTRUCTIONS; DO WHAT THE LABEL SAYS.**

Pest Controls - organic vs. non-organic

Organic controls break down quickly (this is a good thing) and must be reapplied according to a schedule. Synthetic controls typically last longer (have a "residual") and are applied less frequently than organic controls. *Again, read the entire label before using...safety first! Even organic controls kill things.*

SYMPTOM: There are little bugs on the flower spike, bud, and / or flowers.
POSSIBLE CAUSES: Aphids are common culprits found on spikes, buds, and flowers of *Oncidium* Alliance, *Cattleya* Alliance, and *Cymbidium* orchids. You didn't do anything wrong, the aphids just showed up. Aphids suck through a small hole they poke in the plant which can result in malformed flowers and buds.
REMEDY: If you catch this early, and there are just a few aphids, they

Aphids on Epidendrum *flowers*

often can be rinsed off with water. Applying plant oil-based, organic controls (e.g. Neem Oil) and Insecticidal Soap can keep aphid populations in check. Any control, organic or otherwise, when applied to flowers or buds may cause bud blast. Also check to see if any nearby plants have aphids.

SYMPTOM: There are ants crawling up and down the flower spike on my orchid. Should I do anything?

POSSIBLE CAUSES: Ants themselves are not a problem, but the presence of ants on your orchid tells you there is likely another bug present. Ants love the sugary secretions of sucking insects like scale, mealybugs, and aphids.

REMEDY: If you do have other bugs, control the bugs, and the ants go away. Use an appropriate control for sucking insects like a Neem Oil-based product. Read the entire label before using.

SYMPTOM: What is this white cottony fuzz on my plant?

POSSIBLE CAUSES: The dreaded mealybug! Mealybugs can be found almost anywhere on your plant: in the folds of the leaves, on the potting media, side of the pot, flowers, inside unopened flower buds, on the flower spike, or even the stake and tie supporting it. Mealybugs, like aphids, are sucking insects, and they just showed up; you didn't do anything that caused their arrival.

What is this white fuzzy thing on my orchid? The dreaded mealybug!

Mealybugs are especially tough to eradicate, because their "fuzziness" tends to repel liquid sprays. Their ability to hide in folds of leaves and other tight places also makes control challenging.

REMEDY: Keep an eye on your plants so you detect the presence of mealy bugs early on, before they reach epidemic proportions. Mealybugs won't kill your plant right away, but they are very unsightly and can definitely prevent your orchid from reblooming. Check nearby plants for mealybugs.

Keep the leaves of your orchids clean and free of dust. Some people manually remove mealybugs with a cotton swab and alcohol. Organic sprays are available like Neem Oil and Insecticidal Soap. Be sure to read the entire instruction label before using, especially when it comes to reapplication times. Be persistent for total control; you will commonly need to reapply sprays several times to fully eradicate mealybugs.

Check your other nearby plants for mealybugs. If your orchids are growing under a tree, check the tree for mealybugs.

SYMPTOM: I see this white cottony fuzz on the tie that attaches the flower spike to the stake.
POSSIBLE CAUSES: Sounds like mealybugs again. See the previous question.
REMEDY: Remove the tie and stake. Thoroughly clean that part of the plant and see remedy to the previous question.

SYMPTOM: There is this clear sticky stuff on some of the leaves of my orchid.

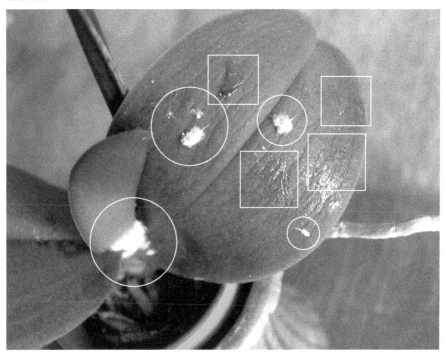

Shiny, clear, sticky residue on leaves (squares) resulting from the sugary secretions of sucking insects, in this case mealybugs (circles).

POSSIBLE CAUSES: The clear sticky stuff is likely the sugary secretion, or "honeydew," of sucking insect pests like aphids, mealybugs, and scale. Or it is possible that somebody spilled something, like fruit juice, on your plant.

REMEDY: The bugs are either on the plant or on a plant above your orchid. Clean the leaves - squirt a little lemon juice (from a lemon!) in a cup of water; dip a paper towel or soft towel in the diluted lemon juice and wipe the leaves clean. Keeping the leaves clean helps you see where if any stickiness re-emerges so that you may focus your efforts in the right place.

Alternatively, organic sprays are available like Neem Oil and Insecticidal Soap. Be sure to read the entire instruction label before using, and be ready to reapply according to the directions.

SYMPTOM: There is this black sooty looking stuff on the leaves of my orchid.

POSSIBLE CAUSES: Lots of things could have fallen on your plants creating the look of black soot, like construction dust, other dust, or overspray from paint.

However, if the black soot feels slightly sticky and easily rubs off with your finger, it could be "sooty mold." Sooty mold is a common fungus that grows on the sugary, sticky secretions of sucking insects like scale and mealybugs. It won't kill the plant, but it will decrease the plants ability to grow by blocking the sun from hitting the leaves.

Again, this is very common. Orchid outdoors can also get sooty mold from sticky bug secretions dropping onto their leaves from the trees or plants above them.

REMEDY: Control the sucking insect, and the sooty mold will die. However, even after you control the bug, you may still need to manually clean the leaves to remove the sooty mold.

SYMPTOM: There are these little brown/black dots or bumps on the leaves of my orchid.

POSSIBLE CAUSES: First, do the bumps easily fall off if you try to remove them? If not, see the question in the previous section on oedema and leaves. If the bumps do fall off, your orchid may have scale insects, another type of sucking insect. Scale somehow seem to find our orchids and other plants from time to time. They look like light tan to brown to black bumps ranging in size from smaller than a sesame seed up to the size of a lentil.

Scale, like other sucking insects, exude a sticky, sugary residue that is sometimes found on the leaves. Scale can be found on both sides of the leaves, flowers spikes, and all parts of a plant. On *Phalaenopsis* orchids, scale like to hang out on the underside edge of the leaf, among other places.

Scale insects on a Cymbidium *leaf (left) and on a* Oncidium *leaf (right).*

REMEDY: Same remedy as for mealy bugs, and aphids: treat plant with an organic control for sucking insects (e.g. Neem Oil); clean plant and remove all visible scale; check nearby plants for scale.

SYMPTOM: There are these tiny little light-colored markings on the leaves of my orchid. Are bugs doing that?
POSSIBLE CAUSES & REMEDIES: A few different bugs and pests can cause light colored makings on orchid leaves. Here again, to be absolutely sure, take your plant to someone and have them look at it. Here are a few possibilities:

Spider mites are teeny, tiny sucking insects that congregate in little webs, often on the undersides of leaves. Their sucking action leaves tiny, little dots or "stippling" on the leaves. Try releasing lady bugs or use an organic control for sucking insects like Neem Oil.

Unlike most pests who randomly discover your orchid treasures, spider mites are often associated with dry plants, dry potting, and/or dry, still air. Be sure the plant is receiving supplemental humidity (see the section on "Humidity" in Chapter 2), located away from heater vents, and is properly watered (see Chapter 4). Hose off the plant to remove all webs, and clean each leaf with diluted lemon juice to remove all spider mites.

Thrips on the other hand create irregular light marks by chewing in little patches on the surfaces of the leaves. Use an organic remedy for chewing insects.

Thrip damage on Dendrobium *leaves.*

SYMPTOM: What's eating these holes in the leaves of my orchid?
POSSIBLE CAUSES: A type of "chewing bug" (i.e. not a sucking insect) like slugs, snails, and caterpillars are the usual culprits when it comes to holes in leaves. In contrast, all "sucking insects" (e.g. aphids, scale, mealy bug, white fly) do not make holes in leaves, nor do they eat pieces of the leaves.

REMEDY: First you will need to figure out what is eating your plant. Controls differ for slugs and snails versus caterpillars versus grasshoppers. Without finding out what is eating your plant you will not be able to select an appropriate control.

Iron phosphate is an effective, certified organic, slug and snail control; it's just a mineral, and it's safe around cats and dogs. It comes with many trade names or brands; just be sure to look for "Iron Phosphate" on the ingredients label.

"Bt" is an organic, biological control that works only on caterpillars. "Bt" stands for the initials of the scientific name of a bacteria (*Bacillus thuringiensis*) that kills caterpillars by interfering with their digestion.

Grasshoppers are a tough one. Most controls are not effective against grasshoppers. Bug netting can be draped over plants when grasshoppers are present. Also, grasshoppers eat on the leaf margins, so they don't make "holes" in leaves, but they can eat quite a bit of leaf area.

For guaranteed success, and before you use any control, read the entire instruction label. Don't just "bomb" your plants. Get informed and be sure to use something that truly suits your needs.

Consider too that it is possible that whatever ate holes in your leaves is gone now, and using any kind of control may be useless. A yellow margin around the eaten portion of the leaf indicates that the damage was not recent.

SYMPTOM: It looks like something is eating (or has eaten) the flowers on my orchid.
POSSIBLE CAUSES: Some kind of "chewing insect" must be present; slugs, snails, caterpillars, or grasshoppers are the usual culprits when it come to holes in flowers or pieces of flowers missing. By contrast, all of the "sucking insects" mentioned above do not make holes in leaves or eat "chunks" out of the flowers.
REMEDY: See remedy to previous question.

SYMPTOM: The leaves on my orchid look like they have little spider webs. What should I do?
POSSIBLE CAUSES AND REMEDIES: Webs from actual spiders are not bad for your orchid; spiders eat bugs. However, webs resulting from *spider mites* should be a concern. The webs of spider mites are very finely textured

and smaller in scale than most spider webs, resembling mist or very fine, see-through fabric.

Webs resulting from an infestation of spider mites. Correct, this is not an orchid plant.

Unlike most pests who randomly discover your orchid treasures, spider mites are often associated with dry plants, dry potting media, and/or dry, air. Be sure the plant is receiving supplemental humidity (see the section on "Humidity" in Chapter 2), located away from heater vents, and is properly watered (see Chapter 4).

Hose off the plant to remove any webs; clean each leaf with diluted lemon juice to remove all spider mites. Try releasing lady bugs or using an organic control for sucking insects like Neem Oil.

SYMPTOM: There are these little black flies resembling fruit flies living in the potting media.

POSSIBLE CAUSES: "Little fruit flies in my potting media," typically points to the presence of fungus gnats. Fruit flies are only found around fruit; no fruit, no fruit flies. Fungus gnats, however, are drawn to constantly moist and/or old, decomposed potting media. They lay their eggs in the potting media, and the developing larvae eat the naturally occurring fungus in the potting media. While they do not directly harm plants, they are a nuisance. Their presence suggests that something is not quite right with the potting media. If their numbers become too large, delicate root tips may be damaged by the larvae.

The presence of fungus gnats indicates you may be watering too frequently and/or need to repot your orchid. Fungus gnats love it when orchid potting media has severely decomposed to a point that it looks like soil and holds a lot moisture in the pot.

REMEDY: The best way to get rid of fungus gnats is to simply repot your orchid at the appropriate time with fresh potting media (see Chapters 2 & 4), and know your plant! Alternatively, you can kill fungus gnat larvae with a "soil drench" in which you water very thoroughly at set intervals with an insecticidal soap. Read all instructions on control before using.

SYMPTOM: I tried using a bug killer for the bugs on my orchid, but it didn't work.

POSSIBLE CAUSES & REMEDY: First be sure that you have positively identified the pest *and* that you have selected a control that lists your pest. If it doesn't list your pest, it doesn't makes sense to spend your money on it.

Read the *entire* instruction label before using; understand (1) how to apply the control, (2) when and when not to apply it, and (3) *how often to reapply it.* Then actually do what the instruction label says to do. Be sure the application covers all parts of the plant, especially the undersides of the leaves.

Many organic controls frequently fail to eradicate all of the pests *the first time.* Organic controls break down quickly, and do not last for long, (that's a good thing!). Therefore, they must be reapplied according to the instructions for guaranteed success, sometimes every 3-4 days.

Also consider that *your pest may now be gone*, and the damage is done. If critters ate holes in your leaves, and the critters are now gone, there is no spray that will make the holes go away.

OTHER PROBLEMS AND QUESTIONS

SYMPTOM: My orchid plant is growing over the side of the pot.
POSSIBLE CAUSES: Sympodial orchids (see Chapter 3) create new growths from a rhizome that cause the plant's overall size to increase over time; they will eventually outgrow their pot, some faster/slower than others. If your sympodial orchid is growing over the side of the pot, it needs to be repotted.

Yes, I am growing over edge of my pot. Pleeease repot me!

Monopodial orchids (see Chapter 3) generally do not create new growths, Instead, they grow leaves one at a time on the top of the plant, growing in one direction, up. Over time monopodial orchids may lean over the side of the pot. Upon repotting, the plant can be re-oriented in a more upright direction as best as possible.
REMEDY: Repot the orchid as described in Chapter 2.

SYMPTOM: My *Phalaenopsis* orchid is leaning over the edge of its pot, OR My *Phalaenopsis* orchid is real wobbly in its pot. Should I do something about it?

POSSIBLE CAUSES: *Phalaenopsis* orchids have a monopodial growth habit (see Chapter 3) which means that they grow in one direction - up. As the plant grows upwards, it may lose a few of the lower leaves; the plant may eventually become a little top heavy and lean over the edge of the pot. In nature, a *Phalaenopsis* orchid would be climbing up the trunk of the tree to which it is attached; hence the tendency to want to lean on something when grown in a pot.

Alternatively, your *Phalaenopsis* orchid may be wobbly or leaning over the edge of its pot, because the roots have rotted in the pot. Once this happens the plant can lose its anchor in the pot.

REMEDY: Your *Phalaenopsis* needs to be repotted at the next appropriate time. Gently take the plant out of the pot and inspect the roots. If the roots look fine and the root mass is so huge that's it's hard to get it back in the pot, you'll need a larger pot. Repot the orchid at the appropriate time, as described in Chapter 2, and re-orient the plant upright as best you can, but lower in the pot with the base of the lowest leaf level with the new potting media. You may need a stake after repotting to stabilize the plant.

If many roots look rotted, repot the plant with fresh potting media as described in Chapter 2. Select a pot size that comfortably accommodates all the roots without a lot of extra space. If a lot of roots are rotted, a smaller pot may be necessary.

SYMPTOM: My *Phalaenopsis* orchid looks like it is making a trunk. OR My *Phalaenopsis* orchid seems like it has a stem in the middle and the leaves seem really far apart.

POSSIBLE CAUSES:

When a *Phalaenopsis* orchid loses its lowest leaves, the stem base takes on the appearance of a trunk, which can develop when:

*Lack of light and/or lack of water causes the lowest leaves to fall off.
*Having not been repotted in a long time, the oldest leaves have fallen off.
*Having been improperly repotted too high in its new pot.
*A combination of the above.

REMEDY: Repot at the appropriate time (see Chapter 2). Be sure you are providing proper light, water, and supplemental humidity (see Chapter 4).

SYMPTOM: There are roots are growing out above the top of the pot. Why are they growing like that? Should I cut them off?

POSSIBLE CAUSES: Most orchids we're discussing in this book are "epiphytic," meaning they live in trees. As epiphytes, roots grow out in all directions looking for something to attach to. Some *epiphytic roots* "stick" to things while *aerial roots* grow in the air. It can therefore be perfectly natural for roots to grow out of the top of the pot.

A lot of roots are growing up over the top of the pot. Should you be concerned?

Healthy orchids that need a larger pot, may grow roots on top of the pot, because there is no more room in the pot.

At the same time, an orchid may make roots *on top of the pot* because it is unhappy *in the pot*. For instance, when an orchid has been overwatered or the potting media has severely decomposed, the roots are likely to rot, resulting in an unhappy plant. The plant compensates by creating new roots in a potentially happier place, *above* the pot.

REMEDY: First, don't cut off those roots! I've found that for some people it is quite the challenge to coexist with these squiggly gray things sticking out of the pot all over the place. There seems to be this impulse to cut them off...please refrain.

Instead, take the plant out of the pot and inspect the roots (see above regarding roots). If roots look fine, put the plant back in the pot and leave it. If the root mass looks healthy and is totally filling the pot, you may need to repot the orchid into a larger pot at the appropriate time (Chapters 2 and 3). Tuck those healthy roots down into the new pot; I like to leave a couple of roots sticking out so I can watch the root tips grow.

However, if the roots look rotted in the pot, you likely need to repot the orchid with fresh potting media, maybe into a smaller pot (see Chapter 2).

Healthy roots should appear firm and grayish-white to whitish-green.

SYMPTOM: The roots of my orchid don't look healthy...I'm not sure if they're healthy...How do I know my orchid's roots are healthy?
POSSIBLE CAUSES & REMEDY: As stated throughout this book and in this chapter, inspecting the roots greatly helps you assess the health of your orchid plant. Healthy roots are firm, grayish-white to whitish-green with a shiny green or reddish green tip. Dead roots are soft and mushy, to dry, hollow and brittle, ranging in color from brown to gray to black.

Roots can die for several reasons: too much water, too cold, too hot, etc. It is common for the some of the oldest roots to die off. On monopodial orchids, the oldest roots are those attached lowest on the central growth. For sympodial orchids, the oldest roots grew from the oldest growths and pseudobulbs (see Chapter 3). If all the roots are rotted, the plant may have been overwatered, and as a result, needs to be repotted.

The presence of some healthy roots greatly increases the chances the orchid plant will recover from its traumatic event. If the roots look ok, replace the plant in its pot, and continue as you have been. Lots of healthy roots on top of the pot may indicate a problem (see previous question).

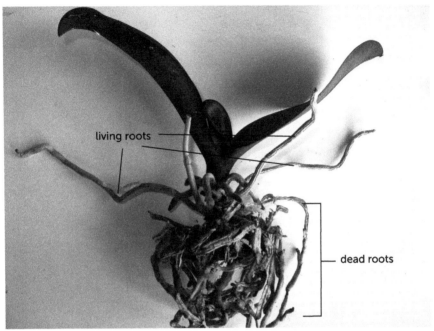

living roots

dead roots

All of the roots that were growing inside the pot are dead. All the roots that were growing on top of the pot are alive. This orchid probably suffered from overwatering, meaning the roots were lacking air, or had not been repotted in a timely manner.

SYMPTOM: The roots of my orchid look like they're green. Is that okay?
POSSIBLE CAUSES: Some orchid roots have a potential to photosynthesize and may have a slightly green cast to them. In clear plastic orchid pots, roots tend to be "greener" than in opaque pots. It is very common for healthy root tips to be bright shiny, light-green.

Then again, algae can grow in clear plastic pots or in pots with fairly decomposed potting media, especially in high-humidity, greenhouse-like settings.
REMEDY: If the roots are healthy and the potting media seems fresh, don't do anything. If the roots are healthy and the potting media needs refreshing, repot when it is a good time to do so. If neither the roots seem healthy nor the potting media is good, repot the orchid but read this chapter from the beginning, and…know your plant!

SYMPTOM: I did what you said and took my *Phalaenopsis* out of its pot. Every single root was rotted and dead. What do I do now?

POSSIBLE CAUSES: The plant could have suffered from being too cold, too wet, not having been repotted in forever, etc.

REMEDY: When your *Phalaenopsis* orchid is totally lacking roots, your goal is to get the plant to grow new roots before it dies from lacking roots. **High humidity is the key to quickly growing roots.**

One technique that I have had success with involves placing sphagnum moss around the base of the plant and putting the whole thing in a clear plastic bag, leaving a small opening in the top of the bag for a small amount of air flow. This high humidity, mini-greenhouse environment may be the best hope for inducing a root or two to grow on a severely stressed *Phalaenopsis* orchid. Occasionally mist the moss; don't let the bag cook in the direct sun.

SYMPTOM: The newest growth, leaves and pseudobulbs, upon maturity, are smaller than previous leaves.

POSSIBLE CAUSES: It is extremely important and perceptive of you to have noticed this. How the youngest leaves look in relation to the older leaves is a powerful tool to help you assess the health of your plant.

When an orchid is unable to grow leaves or pseudobulbs as big as the previous leaves or pseudobulbs, it always means the orchid has been experiencing a less ideal environment than it had been in the past when it grew those larger leaves or pseudobulbs. That is, some essential aspect of the environment in the orchid's native habitat must be missing, e.g. too much light, improper watering, too little humidity (see Chapters 1 and 2).

Furthermore, if an orchid is in desperate need of repotting or has been severely neglected, the new growth upon maturity, is often smaller than previous mature growths. Many "gifted" non-blooming orchids ("it just never rebloomed for me") exhibit this phenomenon.

REMEDY: Be sure that you are providing proper light, water, humidity, etc. (see Chapters 3 and 4, and know your plant!). Repot your orchid at the appropriate time if you have not done so for a few years (see Chapter 2). See also the section above in this chapter on "Problems With Leaves."

Healthy orchids grow new leaves, growths and pseudobulbs that are at least as big if not bigger than previous ones. If this is not happening, some aspect of the orchid's environment needs to be changed.

APPENDIX

Glossary of Orchid Related Terms

References

Acknowledgments

An Aspiration

GLOSSARY OF ORCHID RELATED TERMS

aerial roots - roots that literally grow in the air; common for many epiphytic (tree dwelling) orchids.

alliance - A group of genera with similar characteristics that are capable of interbreeding. For example, the *Cattleya* Alliance includes the genera *Cattleya, Brassavola, Laelia, Sophronitis, Epidendrum*, and more. In botanical taxonomy, an alliance is analogous to the term "subtribe."

axil - The space in the upper angle formed where a branch or leaf joins the stem from which it grew. Many orchid flower spikes emerge in leaf axils.

back bulb - Older or oldest pseudobulbs on an orchid. Back bulbs commonly lack leaves.

bud - The term for a flower that has not yet opened; can also refer to a small, emerging growth.

***Cattleya* Alliance** - A group of genera related to *Cattleya* orchids (e.g. *Cattleya, Brassavola, Laelia, Sophronitis, Epidendrum,* and more), all capable of interbreeding.

charcoal - An orchid potting media additive that provides aeration and absorbs excess salts. Charcoal is made from heated wood, usually hardwood.

clone - A plant produced asexually, i.e. by division, cutting, tissue culture, etc. Any plant created asexually will be genetically identical to the parent plant and have identical flowers.

coconut fiber - The husk of a coconut fruit. It is commonly chopped or shredded and used in potting mixes as a longer lasting and more sustainable peat moss substitute.

coir pith - Finely shredded husk of a coconut or coconut fiber. Used as a peat moss substitute, coir pith holds moisture while providing aeration, but lasts longer than peat moss. Be sure to use the proper grade, from a fine powder, to more chunky bits, depending on the type of orchid.

column - Unique to orchids, the column is the structure resulting from the fusion of male and female reproductive parts in an orchid flower.

cool-growing - One of three temperature growing regimes pertaining to orchids that dislike temperatures over 80F / 27C and require cool nights to thrive and rebloom. Some cool-growing orchids, like *Cymbidiums,* require fall night temperatures under 50-55F / 10-13C to rebloom; others, like *Masdevallia,* simply need cool temperatures all year long.

cross - Hybridization event in which pollen is transferred from the flower of one type of plant to the flower of a different type of plant.

cultivar - With regards to orchids, a cultivar (short for "cultivated variety") is one individual plant grown from seed. A cultivar may be of a species or a hybrid. A cultivar may only be propagated asexually (e.g. division, tissue culture) to remain the same cultivar. Cultivar names are capitalized, in Roman, and contained within single quotes.

deciduous - Describing plants that lose their leaves for a portion of the year.

division - A means of asexual propagation in which the plant is literally split or "divided" into two or more pieces. Many monopodial orchids have only one shoot and cannot to be divided.

dormant - When a plant is not growing. An orchid plant may or may not lose its leaves during this dormancy period.

dorsal sepal - All orchids have three sepals which cover the developing flower bud; when you look at a flower bud you are looking at the three closed sepals. For most orchids, when the flower opens (see "resupinate"), the dorsal sepal points up. The other two sepals point to the side and are called "lateral sepals."

epiphyte - 'Epi' meaning on; 'phyte' meaning plant. Therefore "epiphyte" refers to plants that grow on other plants, like many orchids.

equitant - Referring to leaves that grow "flat" in two ranks in the same plane, like a fan, e.g. *Iris, Gladiola.* With regard to orchids, the genus *Tolumnea* (formerly called *equitant Oncidium*), have no pseudobulbs and thick three-sided equitant leaves. Many *Vanda* relatives have equitant leaves.

evergreen - Describing plants that retain their leaves throughout the year.

family - A group of plants sharing some characteristic. For example, the Orchidaceae is the family of all orchid genera and species.

fir bark - The processed bark of a fir tree, usually Douglas Fir. It is graded into various sizes, can be used alone or in mixes, and has a slightly acidic pH. It holds 60-80% of its weight in water. When really dry, bark needs soaking to fully hydrate it. Be sure to use the correct grade of fir bark that your particular orchid requires.

flower spike - The "stem" (peduncle) that holds the flower buds.

free-blooming - In the most vague, general terms, free-blooming means that the plant blooms "kinda whenever." More specifically, free-blooming refers to orchids that lack a rest period, usually because the conditions in their native habitat remains fairly consistent throughout the year. As a result, they constantly create new growths and bloom "freely" with each new growth.

genus - (pl. genera) A group of similar organisms sharing a common ancestral heritage. The *Genus* name is capitalized and italicized.

grex - the name referring to the seedlings of a specific hybrid or cross. Grex names are capitalized with Roman lettering. For instance, for *Miltassia* Shelob 'Tolkien,' Shelob is the Grex name that refers to all offspring resulting from any cross between *Miltassia* Olmec and *Brassia* Edvah Loo. 'Tolkien' is one seedling (or cultivar - see above) from that cross/hybrid.

growth habit - How a plant grows and what it does over the course of one year.

habitat - The environment in which an organism lives.

humidity tray - A saucer or tray containing wet rocks or a water-filled tray. Orchids are placed *on humidity trays, on top of wet rocks, not in standing water*. The water evaporates from the rocks or tray increasing the humidity of the microclimate around the orchid plant.

hybrid - As the term relates to orchids, an orchid whose parents are different species. "Natural hybrids" occur by natural processes in nature; "artificial hybrids," on the other hand, result from a human moving pollen from one flower to a flower on a different plant.

hygrometer - Instrument or tool for measuring relative humidity.

inflorescence - Referring to the arrangement of flower(s) on one spike (peduncle).

intergeneric hybrid - A hybrid between plants in *different* genera.

intermediate-growing - One of three temperature regimes for growing orchids: typically maintaining ideal temperatures between 55-80F / 13-27C, not too hot, not too cold, depending on the type.

intrageneric hybrid - A hybrid between plants in the *same* genus.

keiki - The Hawaiian word for "baby" or "child" refers to a baby plantlet produced by some orchids on flower spikes (e.g. *Phalaenopsis*) or on pseudobulbs (e.g. *Dendrobium*). Once a few 2-3" long roots have developed, the keiki can be removed and potted separately; it may take a few years for the keiki to bloom.

labellum - Botanical term for the often highly ornate and specialized third petal that hangs down on most orchid flowers, also called the lip. The often decorative and extravagant shapes, colors and textures may appear wavy, pouch-like, frilly, etc. The features of the labellum are designed to lure potential pollinators to the pollen/nectar source. See also "lip."

lateral petal - All orchids have three petals, one of which is typically highly modified and called the "lip" or "labellum." The other two are called "lateral petals" and generally point to each side of the flower.

lateral sepal - All orchids have three sepals which cover the developing flower bud; when you look at a flower bud you are looking at the three closed sepals. When the flower opens, the lateral sepals are behind the three petals and point to the sides from behind the lip. The lateral sepals in a *Paphiopedilum* orchid are fused behind the lip and are called a "synsepalum." The third sepal that points up on most orchids is called the "dorsal sepal."

lava rock - Literally, rock that was once molten lava. Orchids that we see potted in black lava rock were likely grown in Hawaii, where there is plenty of black lava rock. Lava provides excellent aeration, and because it is inert, a balanced fertilizer must be provided. Be sure to use the proper grade of lava rock for your particular orchid.

leaf axil - The area in the upper angle formed where a leaf joins a stem.

lip - The often highly ornate and specialized third petal that hangs down on most orchid flowers; also called the "labellum." The decorative and extravagant shapes, colors and textures may appear wavy, pouch-like, lacy, spotted, etc. The labellum is designed to lure potential pollinators to the pollen/nectar source. The two other petals are called "lateral petals."

lithophyte - A plant growing on rocks; from the Greek: 'litho' = rock, 'phyte' = plant.

maximum / minimum thermometer - A special type of thermometer that records the maximum and minimum temperatures over a given interval of time.

microclimate - Features of the environment in small spaces/scales that differ environmentally from other areas. Many different microclimates are found throughout your home, from home to home, outdoors, and inside greenhouses.

monpodial growth habit - Growth habit predominantly in one direction.

From the Greek 'mono' = one; 'pod' = foot. "walking" in one direction. For monopodial plants, one growth/shoot flowers throughout the life of the plant.

native habitat - describing where a given plant may be found growing wild, in nature.

node - The location where a leaf or stem joins a stem.

non-resupinate - Referring to flowers buds that do not twist 180 degrees as the flower develops and opens. Non-resupinate flowers have a lip that points up (e.g. *Osmoglossum pulchella*). Contrast with "resupinate," in which the lip hangs down. The vast majority orchids have resupinate flowers.

***Oncidium* Alliance** - A group of genera (e.g. *Oncidium, Brassia, Cochlioda, Miltonia, Miltoniopsis,* and more) capable of interbreeding with *Oncidium* orchids and each other.

operculum - the cap at the end of the column that covers the anthers / pollen sacs on an orchid flower.

osmunda fiber - the root mass of the terrestrial *Osmunda* fern. Lesser common now as an orchid potting media than it once was, it is very tough and durable and holds well over 100% of its weight in water.

panicle - A often loosely branched inflorescence in which the flowers open starting from the center or bottom to the top or outer tip of the branches (e.g. *Oncidium*).

peat moss - Decomposed sphagnum moss mined from the bottom of peat bogs. Capable of holding a lot of moisture, peat moss is sometimes added to orchid potting mixes.

pedicel - The technical term for the little stalk or stem *that supports one flower* in an inflorescence. If the flower is pollinated, part of the pedicel will become the ovary where seed develops (fruit).

peduncle - The botanical term for a flower spike or stalk of either one flower or an inflorescence.

peloric - Describing a flower with two lateral petals that appear similar to the lip.

pendulous - With regard to orchids, describing flower spikes that hang down (e.g. some *Cymbidium*) or emerge from the bottom or sides of slatted baskets (e.g. *Dracula*).

perlite - A superheated, volcanic ash mineral often used as an additive to fir bark based orchid potting media. Perlite is an inexpensive, light-weight filler that provides excellent aeration and drainage while providing some water retention.

petal - All orchid flowers have three petals: two lateral petals and a third petal often highly modified and called a "lip" or "labellum."

pollinia - The mass of waxy pollen in an orchid flower.

potting media - As it refers to orchids, any of the various substances used to grow orchids in pots.

primary hybrid - Cross or hybrid made between two different species, as opposed to cross involving a hybrid orchid.

pseudobulb - A primarily water-storing organ occurring only in orchids. Varying greatly in shape and size, pseudobulbs can be egg-shaped to reed-like and range in size from a few millimeters to 10 feet tall!

pumice - Superheated volcanic rock, typically used as an additive in orchid potting media. Pumice is slightly heavier than perlite, but retains moisture better, while providing excellent aeration and drainage.

reed stem - As it refers to some orchids (e.g. *Epidendrum*), a term describing a thin, stem-like pseudobulb.

relative humidity - Relative humidity is not the percentage of water vapor in the air. Instead it is a measure of the percentage of humidity in the air, relative to the maximum amount of water vapor the air could hold at that same temperature and air pressure. So by definition, when it is raining the relative humidity is 100%.

rhizome - A horizontal (or mostly horizontal) stem with new shoots often arising along its length as the rhizome grows.

rockwool - Melted rock that is spun into fibers. Rockwool holds lots of water and air at the same time, and because it is inert, rock wool is best used as an additive to potting mixes.

scape - A leafless peduncle or "stalk" supporting the flower(s) of a stemless plant (e.g. orchid, tulip).

seedling orchid - A young orchid that has yet to bloom.

semi-terrestrial growth habit - Growing not in soil, but in loose substrate like leaf litter.

sepal - All orchid flowers have three sepals. What you see when you are looking at an unopened orchid flower bud are the three sepals enclosing the other flower parts. Many times the color and texture of the three sepals are very similar to that of the two lateral petals; sometimes they are very different. For instance, in the genus *Masdevallia* and *Dracula*, the sepals are what you see as the "flower," and the petals greatly reduced in size to only a few millimeters or much less.

sheathing leaves - Temporary leaves that enclose developing pseudobulbs or flower spikes. Some people like to remove them; some like to leave them. Bugs love to hide in old sheathing leaves.

species - Technically, and in most general terms, a species is a reproductively isolated group of organisms, and is the base unit of taxonomy. The name of the species is lowercase and italicized. When this term is applied to orchids, it is very vague indeed.

specimen plant - A large, mature plant, usually producing an abundance of flower spikes.

sphagnum moss - The fluffy moss that grows on the surface of peat bogs. It is often used to improve moisture retention in bark-based potting media.

spike - The informal term for the "stem" that supports the flowers of a plant. The botanical term for spike is *peduncle*.

stigma - Botanically speaking the stigma is the part of the pistil that receives the pollen. In orchids, the stigma is the sticky, hard-to-see patch on the underside of the column that receives pollen.

subtribe - For orchids, a group of genera capable of interbreeding. Analogous to the term "Alliance."

sympodial growth habit - Growth habit branching in more than one direction. From the Greek 'sym' = together; 'pod' = foot, i.e. "walking together" in many directions. Each new shoot grows from a rhizome or bud on the previous growth, and matures/flowers in one season or less.

synsepalum - In *Paphiopedilum* orchids, the two united or fused lateral sepals that hide behind the flower.

terrestrial growth habit - Growing in loose soil.

tissue culture - Method of asexual propagation or cloning of plants. Cells are taken from the apical meristem and grown in laboratory condition creating potentially thousands of new, genetically identical plants.

tree fern fiber - Long lasting potting media derived from the "trunk" of tree ferns. It provides excellent aeration and resists decay. Tree fern fiber is often cut into slabs for mounting orchids.

Vanda **Alliance** - A group of genera (e.g. *Vanda, Ascocentrum, Renanthera,* and more) capable of interbreeding with *Vanda*.

variety - One specific type of species or subset of a species that differs in some way from the standard members of the species. Variety names are lowercase and italicized. A variety differs from a cultivar in that members of a given variety can sexually reproduce to create more members of that variety. A cultivar, however, may only be propagated asexually via division or tissue culture, for instance.

velamen - The spongy covering around orchid roots specially designed to absorb moisture and nutrients, and then dry out quickly. What we see on the roots of a *Phalaenopsis*, for instance, is the velamen. The thin root is inside the velamen.

warm-growing orchid - One of three temperature regimes for growing orchids: providing warm days around 75-85F / 24-30C, depending on the orchid, and night temperatures that never drop below 60F / 15C.

REFERENCES

Aldrich P., W.E. Higgins, B.F. Hansen, R.L. Dressler, T. Sheehan, J. Atwood (2008), The Marie Selby Botanical Gardens Illustrated Dictionary of Orchid Genera. Comstock Pub. Assoc., Ithaca, New York.

*American Orchid Society website. www.aos.org.

*Berliocchi, Luigi (2000), *The Orchid In Lore and Legend,* Timber Press, Portland, Oregon.

*Cullina, W. (2004), *Understanding Orchids*, Houghton Mifflin, New York.

Dressler, Robert L. (1990), *The Orchids - Natural History and Classification*, Harvard University Press, Cambridge.

Dressler, Robert L. (1993), *Phylogeny and Classification of the Orchid Family*, Cambridge University Press, Melbourne.

Harris, James and Melinda (1994). *Plant Identification and Terminology - An Illustrated Glossary,* Spring Lake Publishing, Spring Lake, Utah.

Hessayon, D.G. (2008), *The Orchid Expert*, Transworld Publishers, London.

Internet Orchid Species Photo Encyclopedia, http://www.orchidspecies.com

Leroy-Terquiem, Gerald and Jean Parisot (1989), *Orchids - Care and Cultivation*, Blandford, London.

Orchid genera abbreviations:
http://www.ravenvision.ca/site/resources/abbreviations.htm.

Orchids, The Bulletin of the American Orchid Society, Coral Gables, Florida.

*Random House Australia (2002), *Botanica's Orchids - Over 1200 Species Listed*, Laurel Glen, San Diego.

*Reinikka, Merle A. (1995), *A History of the Orchid*, Timber Press, Portland.

Rentoul, J.N. (1989), *Growing Orchids - Expanding Your Orchid Collection*, Lothian, Port Melbourne.

Stewart, Joyce (1988), *Kew Gardening Guides - Orchids,* Timber Press, Portland.

White, Judy (1996), *Taylor's Guide to Orchids,* Frances Tenenbaum, Series Editor, Houghton Mifflin Company, New York.

Wikimedia Commons: https://commons.wikimedia.org/wiki/Main_Page

* = Chuck's favorites

ACKNOWLEDGMENTS

I must first thank Bruce Verkist for teaching me more about orchids than any one person. From my college days, I'd like to thank Richard N. Mack, PhD at Washington State University for providing me a truly top notch, quality education. I also must thank Larry Clark for giving me a first class, gardening education and Nyle Verkist for showing me how to *really* grow plants.

There are many people to thank who either greatly assisted in the completion of How Orchids Rebloom or without whom this book may have never come to be: Loren Lockman and the Tanglewood Wellness Center; Ann Rushing; Molly Eckenrod; Janet and Bill White & family; Dani Riggs; Dario Berrini; Mike Hardig, PhD; Judy Fulkerson, Rebecca's (in South Park); blurb.com; Glen Barlow at OrchidWorks; Dean Monroe at Kaleialoha Orchids; Forest in Na'alehu; Fred De Boer and the crew at Mainland Floral; Al & Rob; Patti, Heather and Scott; the San Diego County Orchid Society, The Mt. Baker Orchid Society, and the Hilo Orchid Society. Also, I must thank everyone from my years working at Bakerview Nursery in Bellingham, WA and at Walter Andersen Nursery in San Diego, CA. A special thanks goes to my wonderful sister and niece, Ann and Tobey Klungseth, and their family.

And a general thanks for overall inspiration in life goes out to Tom Koenigsberger; my first chess coach Mr. Drennan; Diamond Jack; Jeremy Silman; Jimmy Valiant; chessworld.net; Brian Tichelaar; Leah Blaschke; Jeff and the Dharma Bum Temple; Alan W. Watts; Paul & Jake Waschke; Steve Perry; the San Diego Chess Club; the Dollhausen family; Larry D. Evans and the Mountain Lake Chess Camp; JP and everyone at Peace Pies, and most of all...The Universe.

AN ASPIRATION

When I first started writing this book, I decided to travel to the big island of Hawaii to talk to the "big guys." I wanted to find out how the big commercial orchid growers did business. What were their tricks for growing orchids? Were there any new varieties out there on the horizon?

In one of my meetings I asked the owner if there were any newer orchid varieties coming out that would be easy to rebloom as houseplants. He instantly started laughing, and naturally I had to ask why. He boldly yet truthfully stated, "I grow disposable home decorations, and I can't be concerned with whether or not they rebloom."

WOW! I instantly understood what he meant. He continued, "I only grow winning orchids. Do you want to know what a winning orchid is to me?" "YES!" I replied. "A winning orchid does three things for me. I need to grow orchids that go from flask to flower within 18 months, have a flower that catches your eye, and grow a flower spike 18" tall or less so that they fit on my shipping racks." DOUBLE WOW!

That was an eye opener for me. Sure, it's all about business, I get that, and that is not likely going to change. But so many orchids are just getting tossed in the garbage when they finish blooming!! My aspiration is that after reading this book you will firmly and undeniably believe that it is so easy to get orchids to rebloom (especially *Phalaenopsis*) that you will have a new life mission that rides alongside but counter to this notion that orchids are disposable home decorations.

Start an Orchid Rescue Club; Place a free ad in a newspaper or on Craigslist like I've done, "Don't toss your unwanted orchids! Call Chuck the plant guy, and I'll pick them up for free!" Something like that.

Orchids don't take up a lot of space, they don't use a lot of water, and they definitely don't need something done to them all the time. Put the right orchid in the right place and they will rebloom! If you've got the space, why not? There are tons of orchids getting tossed right now as you read this!

Once they rebloom, give them to your friends (with a copy of this book!). Donate your rescued orphans to retirement residences, conservatories, or your favorite non-profit organization. You might be even able to start your own backyard orchid growing business. Peace!

NOTES

NOTES